MW00353423

The Ruff Guide
to Trading

The Ruff Guide to Trading

Make money in the markets

By Steve Ruffley

Hh

HARRIMAN HOUSE LTD

18 College Street

Petersfield

Hampshire

GU31 4AD

GREAT BRITAIN

Tel: +44 (0)1730 233870

Email: contact@harriman-house.com

Website: www.harriman-house.com

First published in Great Britain in 2015

Copyright © Steve Ruffley

The right of Steve Ruffley to be identified as the Author has been asserted in accordance with the Copyright, Designs and Patents Act 1988.

Paperback ISBN: 9780857194008

eBook ISBN: 9780857194985

British Library Cataloguing in Publication Data

A CIP catalogue record for this book can be obtained from the British Library.

All rights reserved; no part of this publication may be reproduced, stored in a retrieval system, or transmitted in any form or by any means, electronic, mechanical, photocopying, recording, or otherwise without the prior written permission of the Publisher. This book may not be lent, resold, hired out or otherwise disposed of by way of trade in any form of binding or cover other than that in which it is published, without the prior written consent of the Publisher.

No responsibility for loss occasioned to any person or corporate body acting or refraining to act as a result of reading material in this book can be accepted by the Publisher, by the Author, or by the Employer of the Author.

Dedicated to Arthur Ruffley
1921-2015

Every owner of a physical copy of

The Ruff Guide to Trading

can download the eBook for free direct from us at Harriman House, in a format that can be read on any eReader, tablet or smartphone.

Simply head to:

ebooks.harriman-house.com/ruffguidetotrading

to get your copy now.

About the Author

Steve Ruffley has been involved in the finance industry for 15 years. "If it's trading, then I've done it," is one of his favourite sayings.

Steve's career began placing investments for high net worth clients at PricewaterhouseCoopers. He was quickly hooked on the financial markets. After moving to Gibraltar, he joined the Marex trading graduate scheme.

Later, Steve took the opportunity to risk manage some of the best traders in the business at Refco. This was a high-pressure environment where he had to simultaneously monitor all the major markets and up to 40 trading accounts at a time. At one point in the risk room there were 28 screens for two people.

He then went on to run the live floor at Schneider, where there were around 144 traders. This was at the height of the prop trading boom. Over this period Steve had unparalleled access to the thoughts and strategies of some of the best traders around. He saw some common traits of success and also, more importantly, failure. Putting all this knowledge to use, Steve's next move was to start trading from home. Then, after a few years of lonely but successful trading, he decided that there was more to life.

He decided to turn his hand to education and teamed up with InterTrader (intertrader.com) to become their chief market strategist and head of education. "Those who can, do; those who can't teach," the saying goes. Steve decided to prove he could do both, in real time with real money.

Since 2010, Steve has presented nearly 1000 webinars on all aspects of trading and he has traded at over 150 live events, demonstrating how to make money in real market situations. To prove his teaching worked and in preparation for *The Ruff Guide To Trading*, he publicly traded a £5k trading account to £11k in 90 days.

Steve has also written software for MetaStock (TraderMaker PRO), MT4 and recently the new trading platform of Tradable (iView Charts). His technical analysis has been quoted by the *FT*, Bloomberg, Reuters, *Wall Street Journal*, *New York Times* and many other publications.

Preface

What this book covers

This book is a no-nonsense approach to the real world of intraday trading from someone who has done pretty much every aspect of it.

The focus is how to trade the financial markets on an intraday basis. That is, how to make money from short-term moves that happen as part of everyday market activity. Everything in this book relates to trading when the markets are open and identifying short-term trading opportunities.

I have a fairly simple basic rule for understanding market movement. This is that the markets move 80% of the time due to technical trading and analysis, and that the other 20% of the time moves are due to new fundamental news and data. I will cover the fundamental and technical aspects of trading that are vital in getting the right balance for your trading outlook.

There's quite a bit of theory to go through before I get to some practical trading strategies. This is all designed to open your mind to how the markets function and how other traders make money – and therefore how you can make money.

There is a certain mindset you need to adopt when trading. People often refer to this as "trading in the zone." In order to be in the zone you have to first locate the zone and more importantly identify the makeup of your own zone. This is different for different people. You need to understand yourself, other market participants and the trading world in general before you will ever get close to being able to trade in the zone. I'll guide you towards that mindset.

Who this book is for

This book is for anyone who wants to learn the theory and practice behind successful intraday trading. Perhaps you have tried intraday trading before, but you haven't had the success you wanted. Or maybe you have an interest in trading, but aren't sure how to get started. My Ruff Guide is for you.

This is not a book for those who want to get rich quick. If you think this is possible then you will never be able to approach trading the right way, so my ideas are not for you.

A basic knowledge of technical analysis concepts and terms will be helpful, as I do not go into detail on these. There are many beginner's books on technical analysis available, as well as free resources on the internet.

How this book is structured

The book begins with some high-level theory that you need to know. Unfortunately without understanding this initial chapter, you won't be able to take your trading further and the rest of the book will be of little use.

The focus moves on to fundamental and technical perspectives of how the market functions and how you should position your strategies as a trader.

I will then discuss the importance of having a trading plan, or at least some goals for what you are realistically trying to achieve. Without this you will soon get disillusioned and will not make the best use of your time within the markets.

From there I move on look at three practical strategies you can use in your own trading. It is important that you follow the book in order – there is nothing to be gained from skipping sections.

Contents

Introduction

MY NAME IS STEVE RUFFLEY. I AM A PROFESSIONAL TRADER, risk manager and mentor. I'm not out to prove that I am the world's best trader. What I am trying to prove is that I can help any level of trader gain that essential trading edge.

The trading landscape has changed over the years, with more and more people gaining access to the financial markets. What has not changed is the type of people who trade the markets professionally and also the way the markets essentially function.

Over the last 15 years, I have learnt a lot about all aspects of trading. From trading my own account, risk managing and mentoring traders, to creating software and signals. If you have ever thought about gaining an edge in trading, believe me so have others. The chances are I've tried it with varying degrees of success.

So my advice is to save yourself the time, money and stress it's taken me to learn the lessons I have. Instead, follow the simple and accessible steps in this book.

Your aim as a developing trader should be to achieve a high-level understanding of people. People control every aspect of what happens in the world of trading to some degree. Understand people and you will understand the markets.

Everything you read here is taken from my own experience. If it is in the book it is because it has either made me money or lost me money. *The Ruff Guide to Trading* is an accumulation of thousands of hours of trading, charting and teaching.

My methods of teaching traders are to give them the building blocks to establish their own opinions, strategies and confidence. There is no shortcut to learning the art of trading, but the process can be sped up by a good guide and the right approach to learning.

Let's get started.

PART 1.
Theory and Understanding

CHAPTER 1.

Trading FAQs

Introduction

ONE OF THE WAYS I TEACH TRADING IS VIA INTERACTIVE webinars. I have presented around 1000 over the last five years. This generates a lot of questions, as people are able to put these to me directly. I always state that there are no bad questions regarding trading – if you need to ask something, do so, as what's the worst that can happen?

So, here are the most common questions I am asked by ordinary people on the subject of trading. Depending on your level of experience some questions will be relevant now and some will become more relevant to you later.

We all see the markets in our own way and there is never one definitive answer to most questions. The point of these commonly asked questions is for you to get an idea of what you know, what you think you know and what you may have never considered.

Understanding your actions by continually asking yourself questions is one of the most important routines you can get into as a trader. If you have never asked yourself or an experienced trader some or all of these questions, the chances are that you have not been trading to your full potential.

1. Why do people trade the markets?

This is an easy starter for 10. People trade to make money! Or at least that is the general consensus.

The markets exist to facilitate trade. People seek to find the most efficient way to achieve their goals. These goals to a large extent do not always start out being solely related to money, but invariably money becomes a factor in facilitating them.

People invented money, the markets and everything in-between. Understand people and you will begin to understand how and why the markets function the way they do.

2. How do you, Steve Ruffley, trade the markets?

My 80/20 rule of trading really explains a lot about how I believe the markets function.

In my experience, the market will move 80% due to traders making calls on technical analysis and 20% of the time due to fundamental reasons.

Here's a summary of my process:

1. I understand what has happened in the past to predict future movement – **80% technical analysis**.

2. I study the underlying opinions on data, news and sentiment to find out what traders may be basing their calls on – **20% fundamental analysis**.

3. I understand how to identify value in a market and how long it will be available on an intraday basis.

4. I set a risk amount (in money) that I am willing to lose against a reward amount to prove my opinion is correct or incorrect.

3. What are your sources for new information that is not on the charts?

Fundamental analysis is very important. It not only gives you a sense of the bigger picture relating to underlying sentiment but also an opportunity to trade scheduled market moving data events. These scheduled key data events take place every week. Some are more important than others. Economic calendars providing details of scheduled data releases are readily available online.

Aside from the scheduled economic data releases, there is also unexpected news and information which occurs as a result of spontaneous events.

You should look at certain news sources for breaking news, as credibility is key. Here are the sources I use:

Scheduled data events

1. **FXStreet** (fxstreet.com) **economic calendar**. This is good for release times, which are very important when applying the time zone of the data to your own time zone. It is also very easy to filter for key events and by country.

2. **Bloomberg** (bloomberg.com) **economic calendar**. The ranges and expectations on Bloomberg hold more weight and credibility in the markets than those from most other news agencies. I use these as the foundation for my opinions and also to gauge what the true market expectation is likely to be.

Non-scheduled news events

1. **A squawk service**. I use Live Squawk (livesquawk.com) as I know and respect the team behind it. This allows me to hear market moving information in as close to real time as I need.

2. **Any credible and accountable news source, such as**:

   - Bloomberg
   - Reuters
   - Sky News
   - BBC News
   - The Associated Press

Any news service which has a reason to be credible and accountable is useful. This is why I don't trade on the basis of Twitter rumours.

You have to ask yourself the question, "Will other people trade based on this information?" If they won't, it's of no use to you.

4. How much money do I need to deposit to start a trading account?

I usually respond to this with a series of questions:

1. How much per month do you want to return?

2. What are you looking to achieve from trading? Financial independence, replacing your job, a hobby or just a punt?

3. How much do you think you need?

The answers to all of this are covered in the planning chapter. A lot of people would say "How much can you afford to lose?" But that is fairly meaningless. If you set out with this mindset in trading then you will lose that money.

Money you can afford to invest is another matter. In reality, if you are looking to get a decent return and to stay in a trade for any reasonable amount of time then an account size of £5k is a good starting point.

5. How long will it be before most people are profitable?

In my experience it takes around 6-12 months to be comfortable with your trading style and understanding of the markets. This is being able to view the markets technically, understand the fundamental sentiment and be able to place trades with adequate risk and reward. Anything less than that and you are doing well.

This varies from trader to trader. The usual journey is that you make money at the start as you are focused and excited, you then get complacent and lose some money, you then become disillusioned and impatient and spiral out of control, blowing up your trading account. Sound familiar?

It may take you a few attempts and a few blown trading accounts to find your rhythm. Strap yourself in, as trading is all about the long game and planning to achieve your own realistic targets.

6. What technical indicators do you use?

I first and foremost look at indicators the average retail trader would use. I do this to benefit from the self-fulfilling nature of technical analysis. If the majority of traders look at a 20 period moving average to make a call on the market, then it is likely to work in some respect as an indicator. It doesn't mean however that I use these indicators solely to make my actual calls.

I use indicators to get an idea of what the market expects to happen based on what traders can see. I then use a combination of indicators, chart patterns and understanding of fundamentals to make an actual call.

The self-fulfilling prophecy is pivotal when understanding the retail trader versus professional trader mindset. If I know retail traders (the masses) are looking at certain indicators to make calls, I also know that professional traders are looking at those same indicators to potentially manipulate them in the short term for a gain.

The main day-to-day indicators I use for my trade calls and understanding of market movements are:

1. **Fibonacci** – retracements and expansions.

2. **Bollinger Bands** – 20 period.

3. **RSI** – relative strength index.

That's it. Less is more when you are setting up your charts. It's tempting to put lots of indicators on your charts, but don't. If you do not look at a specific indicator at least every hour to judge how the market is moving then it is of no use to your trading strategy moving forward. And how can you look properly at ten or more different indicators every hour? You can't.

7. What time frames do you use for trading?

I use all the time frames available. People generally don't like this answer. It is essential that you use the correct time frames for your technical analysis and also for your intraday trading. These are different so it means you have to use all the time frames available.

The higher time frames are the monthly (MN), weekly (W1) and daily (D1). They are significant as they show me the opens and closes, and highs and lows. Once closed they form a clear reference point for what has happened in the past and therefore what can potentially happen in the future. I use these points as my significant points of interest – basically support and resistance lines.

For trade calls I look at the hourly (H1), 15 minute (M15) and 5 minute (M5) charts. Do not be tempted into building your calls from tick data or 1 minute charts. Just because you want to trade intraday, you don't need to look at the smallest time frames available. You need to look at a reasonable amount of data and build up areas of interest rather than using exact prices.

From the hourly signals I can view my trade unfolding on the M15 and M5 charts. This means I have the ability to see the trade form in a series, confirming smaller time frame candle closes.

Example

Here is an example of trying to go long GBP/USD based on the H1 chart, but viewing this unfold from the M15 and M5 perspective.

CHART 1: GBP/USD ON THE H1, M15 AND M5 CHARTS

Notes:

1. From the H1 view I see two up hourly candles but have the potential to miss exiting the trade on the high point due to the candle closing sharply towards the low.

2. The M15 chart shows seven consecutive up candles, giving me much more opportunity to get long, stay long and take profit at the top.

3. The M5 chart shows the start of the up move and the consolidation (or short-term profit-taking), before another series of seven consecutive up candles extending to the highs.

Using this combination of time frames allows me to build up confidence and hold correct trades for longer. This is a perfect example of intraday trading, buying low and selling high (relative to the H1 and M15 highs).

For me it is key to remember that every four M15 closes I will get another H1 signal. If I can hold four up candle closes on the M15 and get a confirming H1 bullish signal I can potentially get more profit from the trade.

If you can factor this simple statement into your intraday trading you will have a much better chance of holding winning trades.

Don't worry if you are not familiar with everything I have discussed in this short example – there will be more explanation of these ideas later.

8. What is your risk-reward ratio? What ratio should I use?

This is a tricky one. There is no blanket answer as it depends on the individual's trading size, risk appetite and experience. My own risk-reward ratio is not relevant to you. After 14 years of trading it is more a case of do as I say, not as I do.

Risk-reward ratios have never been an issue for me personally. I knew how much I wanted to make in monetary terms and how much I was willing to lose. I have always understood myself and more importantly I have always been comfortable talking in cash money terms for my trades. This is how I understand risk, but it is not the same for everyone.

What is right for you

My main problem when I started trading was the amounts I made never seemed enough. This led me to taking huge risks that were simply unsustainable. I was trading day to day rather than having a long-term strategy.

This is why I teach people a risk framework, risk-reward ratios and how to identify what is right for them. I am much better at teaching risk with a risk manager's hat on rather than a trader's hat, and this is why I am so successful in teaching people to trade. These are two very distinct skills that I have acquired and have taken years to master.

The general rule of thumb is that your risk-reward ratio should be 2:1. This means for every 1 unit of money traded you should look to double it. Or simply put, risk £1 to be rewarded £2 and scale this up.

This goes hand in hand with the industry standard 1% rule of trading risk. If you risk 1% of your total capital on each individual trade this will be a sustainable overall risk strategy. Or so the experts say.

I highlight these generally received 'rules' mainly to show that in the modern markets it's not only impractical but potentially very detrimental to follow them. This attitude to risk is one of the main reasons many retail traders fail. They allow themselves to be directly at the mercy of the professionals by following this rule.

You have to set your own trading rules. This is what 'The Ruff guide to risk' will teach you later.

9. What is your trading strategy?

My strategies all revolve around figuring out what happened in the past and trying to use that to predict the future.

I look to buy low and sell high. I use the indicators for an idea of what the market is anticipating and trade with them when they are working and against them when they are not. I balance out the 20% fundamental news and data with the 80% technical framework I have developed to seek out short-term value.

It is amazing how that simple and obvious statement is soon forgotten in trading. You see retail traders try so often to reinvent trading and find a new edge. It simply does not exist. Trust me, do the basics well and you will be a much happier person and save yourself a lot of time!

I try not to get too hung up about being right. Having an opinion can be an expensive luxury in trading. In my chief market strategist role when I am being quoted by Bloomberg, the *FT* or other news agencies, I want to be right. I want to say something that will come true in time. When I'm trading I just want to make money. Real trading is not about being right. It is about being right at the right time and banking profit.

I will go over three tried and tested strategies in the second part of the book. Do not be tempted to skip to that part without reading the rest. If you take shortcuts now you will pay for it later.

Have these questions raised any questions for you?

1. How many of these questions have you ever thought about and never asked?

2. Do you think your trading experience would have benefited from knowing the answers to some or all of these questions prior to starting out?

3. Is it a coincidence that the same questions come up time and time again?

After presenting thousands of webinars and many mentor sessions speaking to retail traders, I can tell you that these questions are a true insight into the sort of things trading beginners ask and think about.

Now let's move on to the second part of the theory section, looking at how to achieve an understanding of your fellow traders. Understand people and you will go a long way to understanding the markets.

CHAPTER 2.

Understanding People and Yourself

1. People – human version 1.0

WE ARE NOT MAKING A NEW TYPE OF HUMAN BEING; WE ARE still very much man/woman V1.0. As cavemen we wanted the best potential mate, shelter, food and all the other prehistoric luxuries of that time. Have we really changed that much?

Have a think about how humans have evolved through time. Now do the same, taking out the element of money. People's ideals have changed but basic human nature has not.

These days people generally have a lot more of everything, but essentially it's just stuff. Possessions. Our basic needs and purpose is to want what is best for our family, friends and ultimately ourselves. Human beings are intrinsically selfish and driven by the primal desire to protect themselves and loved ones, and to do more and have more. This does not make us bad, it makes us human. It is also one of the reasons we are the dominant species on the planet.

In modern terms, protecting yourself and providing for your family is done with money. The demand to make money, succeed and be happy is man's ultimate goal and it is not changing any time soon.

This is one of the key things to understand when trading. People are more or less the same as each other, and people move the markets.

2. Traders are people too... sort of

I have met literally every type of trader personality imaginable during my years in the industry. From the scam artists, to deluded idiots to the quiet geniuses, I have talked to them all. You quickly start to see some common traits in the traders who will make it and those who will not.

Traders after all are sort of just people, aren't they? I say sort of because they do have that basic set of human needs, but some elements of their personality and psyche do make them very different to the average person. They still have all the underlying desires I mentioned above, but they go about achieving them in different ways.

Traders have reached a mindset that puts them outside the thinking of the average person. To be at the top in trading you have to sometimes sacrifice certain things that are the norm. In my case this was friends outside of trading, long-term relationships and short-term financial security. There was very little room for anything that didn't involve trading.

When you give up these things you have to justify it with the possibility of earning large sums of money and also the self-justification that in the future all these current sacrifices will be worth it.

This is the lifestyle choice and the mindset most top professional traders get into at some point in their career. They will do whatever it takes to win.

There is a reason anyone is a professional at anything, from sports to modelling. Trading is just the same. There are people out there that have invested more time, effort or money. They have simply sacrificed more and therefore those few will reap the greatest rewards. Fact.

Can you say that you have done the same or are potentially willing do this?

No? Well, that's good, as you are not a professional trader. Luckily we are simply trying to emulate their best qualities.

3. Understanding yourself

You are a person but you are probably not a trader, in mindset anyway.

You want the money. You also want the family life and the stability of a guaranteed income. You want a pension, a boss, a mentor and you want a work-life balance. You do not get this being a professional trader.

The reality

The reason professional traders make more money than retail traders is that they have taken the next step in their thinking and trading evolution. They look like us, they think like us, but crucially they don't act like us. Especially under pressure.

This is why we have to set achievable goals. If you put the recommended £5k into an account, read my book and watch a few webinars, do you think you have invested enough to allow you to make hundreds of thousands of pounds trading the markets like the professionals?

How much would you be happy with? 10% a month? £6k a year? More? Less?

If you want to be a trader you have to find your own mindset and rules that will allow you to achieve your goals. Forget about what you can't control. Focus on what will allow you to make the return you think is achievable in the time scales you set.

How I 'got it'

I was told very early on in my career, "Trading is just a game and money is the way to keep score of who is winning."

That mindset worked for me. What we now need to do is get you into the correct mindset as a person and as a trader.

4. Preparing for the trading game

Once you open a trading account and start to trade, it is now you against the world. There are no second chances and very little room for error. Like it or not, if you do not get into this mindset, the dog eat dog way of thinking, you will lose some or maybe all of your money.

You do not have to become a bad person. What you have to do is know and respect your trading enemy. Trading is a faceless war fought over charts and trading screens.

This is the transitional period where you start from the idea that we are all the same, motivated by money. You understand that other people are better at trading than you and more equipped to make money than you, but there is a very small place for the retail trader to be profitable.

It's not all doom and gloom! I can help you cut out the most common mistakes new and inexperienced traders make. You have to be realistic, however, and accept that trading is a tough skill to master.

Learn not to take losses personally, but also accept you can win from trading and that you have just as much right to be in the markets as anyone else. Do not get sucked into the 'imposter syndrome'. The markets exist so that anyone can use them.

Follow my structured and proven way to learn how to interact with the markets, understand yourself and how to trade.

5. Common professional trader myths

Let's get rid of some of the common misconceptions about professional traders.

They are highly intelligent

This plays a part in being a successful trader but not as much as you may think. The ability to remain rational and calm is much more of a key attribute than intelligence in the majority of successful traders I have encountered.

They have access to insider knowledge

There may be elements where professional traders pay for news subscriptions or for access to certain information that is not available to the general public. I can say hand on heart that of all the traders I have met, only a few have ever been told something under the radar that may be of some use to them.

We all know insider trading goes on – people get access to information they should not. This all goes back to the nature of people and traders. If they can get an edge they will use it against you and the markets for their own gain.

However, illicit dealing is so infrequent in my experience that I choose to ignore it. You have to concentrate on what you can control. That is your trading style, risk-reward ratio and your own interaction with the markets. Trading is too difficult to worry about what the next guy does or does not know.

They always make money

As a risk manager I have seen more people lose in trading than succeed. I think the ratio for professional traders is that about 1-in-20 will fail in under a year.

They have the advantage of starting with a lot more money

Yes and no. You need a certain amount of money, but more important is the time; professionals have to dedicate their lives to trading. You can make a good living with a relatively small sized account if you have low living and working costs.

The reason it's tough to be a professional trader is that desk fees are around £2.5k a month and then you have all the other costs of trading on top.

Think of professionals in other areas

Like most things in life, balance is important. Professionalism pays. You can't be too impulsive, but you can't be too cautious. You can't be arrogant, but you can't be unconfident. You need to strike the right balance of personality traits and how you want to interact with the markets.

Take some examples of well-known sports starts. Who has made more money and had more success? The charismatic, unpredictable genius Alex Higgins, or the quiet, robotic Stephen Hendry? The golfer John Daly, or Tiger Woods? The footballer Lionel Messi, or Paul Gascoigne?

I could go on but I think you get my point. I have found that in trading – as in other areas of life – you can be the personality, the maverick, or you can have success. Few do both. In the trading world, it is said there are old traders and there are bold traders. There are no old, bold traders.

Traders are always battling with their ego. From this point onward, you have to try to understand who you are in terms of trading. What do you want to achieve and how do you want to be perceived in the markets? Put this into the context of trading and more importantly how you will make money from it.

CHAPTER 3.
My 80/20 Rule

WHAT IS MY 80/20 RULE? WHY SHOULD YOU FOLLOW IT?

The markets have to continually move while they are open. If they do not move then no one in the industry – traders, hedge funds, IFAs, banks, clearing houses, even the publisher of the *FT* – makes any money. Nobody wants that.

In my experience traders will usually base their decisions and trade calls on some sort of technical analysis. The reason for this is that the charts, indicators and oscillators are the main gateway into viewing the markets. They are the visual representation of what a particular asset class or market has done in the past and therefore what it may do over a specific period of time in the future. In my experience that accounts for 80% of all market movement.

The other 20% of the time the markets move because people are trading based on news, economic data and other underlying sentiment.

To be a complete intraday trader you have to be aware of both sources and trade using both. This is my 80/20 rule of trading.

If you only trade fundamentally, you will not physically be able to place enough trades to make enough money from trading. This is unless you use a lot of size and margin, meaning a few very high-risk trades.

If you trade only technically and always discount sentiment and the fundamentals, you will eventually take a very large loss. I have seen it happen many times.

In the next couple of chapters I will look at the two components of the 80/20 rule in turn.

CHAPTER 4.
My 80/20 Rule – Overview of 20% Fundamental

I WILL START THE EXPLANATION OF MY 80/20 RULE BY LOOKING at the fundamental side as this is something that people often find the most difficult to incorporate into their day-to-day trading activity. When I say fundamentals, I mean any new information that is released or broadcast over the news wires or other media.

This can be key comments from policy makers such as Janet Yellen from the US Federal Reserve talking about interest rates. Or it can be new economic data released from government agencies such as the United States Bureau of Labor Statistics. It can also be major world events, such as terrorist attacks or natural disasters.

Depending on the perceived impact of this fundamental data on the markets, a shift will occur in the supply and demand of certain asset classes, which will cause a subsequent price movement.

Trading fundamental information will give you a potential framework of events to base your trading day, week and month on. It can also give you the conviction to make money. All the biggest winners I have had over the years – and the biggest winners I've witnessed among other traders – have been based on trading some sort of fundamental news.

If you don't want to trade the fundamental data that is fine, but you should always be aware of it. Even if you are trading purely technically, the markets may move unexcitedly against your position due to fundamental data and you need to be aware of what is happening.

Overview of good and bad fundamental news

The table below provides a basic summary of how the markets will generally behave when highly credible, quality information is released.

Good news	Bad news
Demand for the main indices (S&P, FTSE, DAX) will go up.	Demand for the main indices (S&P, FTSE, DAX) will go down.
If the news is area specific the demand for the native currency of the event will go up.	If the news is area specific the demand for the native currency of the event will go down.
Government bonds will decrease in demand.	Government bonds will increase in demand.
Demand for gold and other safe haven currencies like the Swiss franc will decrease.	Demand for gold and other safe haven currencies like the Swiss franc will increase.
Examples	**Examples**
Lowering – cut – of interest rates.	Raising – hike – of interest rates.
Unexpected rise in company earnings.	Unexpected drop in company earnings.
Increase in government fiscal stimulus.	Decrease in government fiscal stimulus.
End of war or civil conflict.	Outbreak of war or civil conflict.
New medical or scientific discoveries.	Reports on harmful effects of consumer products.

Use this grid as a rule of thumb as you watch out for the key events I discuss below. If you watch the markets as the news and data is released, you will be able to identify trends and patterns in how the markets react.

Why new information moves the markets

How and why new information moves the market is explained by the efficient market hypothesis (EMH).

The efficient market hypothesis states that it is impossible to beat the market because existing share prices always incorporate all relevant information. According to the EMH, stocks always trade at their fair value, making it impossible for investors to either purchase undervalued stocks or sell stocks for inflated prices. As such, expert stock selection or market timing cannot deliver outperformance and the only way to achieve higher returns is to purchase riskier investments.

This is one of the cornerstones I was taught as a young trader. Everything known was already priced into the markets. Traders have all the information needed at any point in time to buy, sell and form an efficient market. Only new information would cause this to change.

In a perfect world where everything was equal, this would be achievable and give all market participants a level playing field.

However, theories like the efficient market hypothesis are a great example of how things get glorified in the trading world. The markets are actually fairly simple when it comes to news. The news either matters in that moment or in the immediate short term, or it doesn't.

If it does matter then you will see a movement in a number of markets as this information is traded according to its severity and nature; if it is bullish (dovish in comments) or bearish (hawkish) then these are fairly short lived unless they are of key significance, like an unexpected change in interest rates. If it is just a rumour then it is usually localised to one market at a time.

If money can be made from a specific piece of new information then it will be jumped on by traders. It is that simple. If it's not going to make me a buck then who gives a (insert your own ending). Your job is to pick out some events and learn how you can profit from them.

RUFF TIP

One of the main points to stress around the topic of fundamental information is that you have to quantify it. You have to figure out if it's reliable, if it's important and what it will do to the markets.

When it comes to the internet and especially social media like Twitter, the thing to remember is that there is very little regulation. This means that not all new news is either relevant or even correct. You have to know what information will actually be used by traders. If traders won't use the information then the markets will not react.

What data to look out for

There are three main types of news that are worth trading. The sources I use for this news can all be found back in chapter one, FAQ 3:

1. **News events** – market-moving global events, such as terrorist attacks or acts of God.

2. **Scheduled economic releases** – such as nonfarm payrolls.

3. **Central bank key speakers** – commentary from policy makers such as Mario Draghi (European Central Bank), Mark Carney (Bank of England) and Janet Yellen (Federal Reserve).

1. News events

Newsworthy events are generally things outside the world of trading and economics. These are things like a potential outbreak of war, a terrorist attack or a natural disaster, such as the Fukushima incident in Japan in March 2011.

The impact of these events can be huge, as they make global headlines and impact all markets.

The good news and bad news grid above is a good way to understand these events. Basically, buy gold and sell the major indices on bad news (and vice versa, although sadly there are very few worldwide breaking news events that are good news).

2. Scheduled economic releases

These are the backbone of the fundamental trading month. As I have explained, all economic release data is scheduled and readily accessible. Every country around the world will have scheduled economic data releases and they will generally, depending on the source you use, be ordered or highlighted as to their importance.

A key point is to know what economic cycle we are in. Data falls into two main categories: growth and inflationary. Back in the mid-2000s, we had relatively favourable employment and growth, so we were concerned with inflation. It was all about price stability and making sure that inflation did not erode the money people had to spend.

After the credit crunch of 2007-2009 we were in a different economic cycle. We were suddenly concerned with growth, or any sign of growth to stimulate the economy. Having kept interest rates artificially low inflation was high, but this was a price that had to be paid to stimulate growth.

Then by 2014 we were once again less focused on growth and more interested in interest rates. This meant we had entered another inflationary data cycle.

Once you know what cycle the economy is in, you can then focus on the figures that matter. If we are in a growth cycle then the focus is on figures such as the nonfarm payrolls (the measure of new jobs created in the US economy) and GDP. If we are in an inflationary cycle then the focus is on PPI and CPI (producer/consumer price indices – the measures of inflation), leading into interest rates.

The following table provides a summary of what data to look at in the growth or inflationary stages. These are all figures I have traded live and made money from:

Inflation	Growth
Consumer price index (CPI)	Nonfarm payroll (NFP)
Producer price index (PPI)	Gross domestic product (GDP)
BoE Monetary policy (MPC)	Retail sales
Fed meeting (FOMC)	University of Michigan consumer sentiment index
ECB Minutes	
	Philadelphia Fed
	Consumer sentiment
	Durable goods

Professional traders and others that move the markets will look at all of the above. This means the markets will respond to these data releases.

RUFF TIP

The good thing about scheduled data releases is that they give structure to your trading week or month. If you know there are, for instance, five key pieces of data out that month you can schedule your trading activity around this. Rather than just looking for an intraday trade, you can make sure you build your trading plan around this potential market-moving data.

What data counts?

I always look to the US. Generally speaking, as the US is the largest consuming nation on earth, any data that comes out of America will have some impact on the majority of the major markets.

The USD is still the world's reserve currency and global commodities are priced in USD. The US GDP per capita is around $46k, whereas in China (reportedly now the largest economy in the world) it's around $7k. Also, the US still has the largest and most powerful defences in the world. So realistically, while all this remains in place, the US is the country I will be following economically.

Key data releases do not come much bigger than the nonfarm payrolls (NFP), so let's look at that in more detail.

Nonfarm payrolls (NFP)

The NFP data is researched, recorded and reported by the US Bureau of Labor Statistics and is intended to represent the total number of paid US workers in any business, excluding the following:

1. Government employees.

2. Private household employees.

3. Employees of non-profit organisations.

4. Farm employees (this is why it is called the nonfarm payroll).

Each month the **Current Employment Statistics (CES) program** surveys approximately 144,000 businesses and government agencies, representing approximately 554,000 individual worksites, in order to provide detailed industry data on employment, hours and earnings of workers on nonfarm payrolls.

With such a huge survey, the NFP is notoriously difficult to predict. I have been trying to predict this figure for the last 14 years and I've rarely got it exactly right. Over the last five years, as chief market strategist for InterTrader, I have been asked to comment on the figure publicly a number of times and I have very rarely got it spot on, although I've certainly come close a few times. I think the main point from this is that you shouldn't try to predict the figure at all – you don't need to.

Unlike most other educators, I trade this figure live in front of an audience. I have made more money trading the NFP when it was outside of my own and other market commentators' trading ranges than when I was close. What you can guarantee is that there will be volatility and market movement around the NFP, which for intraday traders presents a good opportunity to enter short-term trades.

NFP trading example

When you are trading data releases it is important to use the correct time frame to combine the fundamental data that is moving the markets with your technical analysis. The first M5 spike and M15 close are very important when trading a fundamentally-driven move and getting confirmation of its true direction.

This example reiterates how important it is to prepare in advance, and understand your technical analysis and fundamental principles. I made money from this trade and this was down to understanding my 80/20 principles as a whole and having confidence in my trading strategy.

When an NFP release is due, the market will have an estimated consensus figure in mind. In December 2014 the forecast was 240k. There is generally a range of expectation put on this estimate, for example a low of 200k and a high of 290k.

A good figure – better than the consensus forecast – will create demand for the major indices and send the price up. The opposite will happen for safe havens like gold and the Swiss franc; there will be less immediate demand and the price will go down.

In this instance, the actual figure came in at 353k, so 113 points better than forecast. Chart 2 is a 15 minute gold chart after the December 2014 NFP figure was released. This figure was well above the consensus range so in the eyes of the trading world this was a huge sell for gold.

However, the big players, market makers, institutions and trading robots did not let this happen. Gold rallied in two separate movements (the up arrows) over 84 ticks. This is more risk than any retail or indeed hardened professional trader could take if they had gone short on the back of this very positive data.

CHART 2. GOLD AT THE TIME OF NFP RELEASE

Gold was then pushed to a high of 1207.68 over the course of the next 30 minutes of trading. It then made a small attempt to take profit at the top of the range for 15 minutes.

It was only 45 minutes after the NFP release that the expected and true movement on gold emerged: a sell off. Gold then sold off relentlessly for 200 ticks.

You can believe whatever reason you like for this. It is a fact that the market knows people will sell gold on a very high NFP figure. Remember the figure was 113 points better than the consensus and for the NFP this is massive. Between 1203.55 and 1207.68 we saw a fundamental short.

RUFF TIP

A key lesson to learn is that professional traders use what other traders expect to happen against them in the short term.

Large banks, institutions and the markets in general can use the NFP or any other key data for manipulation. In this instance of the good figure, everyone knew that gold should go down. So gold went up past the 1% to 2% risk-reward margin for the average trader, and stopped them out.

Four M15 closes or one H1 candle later, gold saw a significant sell off. Retail traders lost out, professional traders won more.

It's not always about fastest finger first. Weigh up the data and the technicals. There will always be a second wave of movement and an opportunity to make money after the release.

---

3. Central bank key speakers

There are few other events that move the markets like unexpected or previously unreleased comments from the Federal Reserve (Fed), European Central Bank (ECB) and Bank of England (BOE). It is important to listen to the elected heads of state like President Obama, but when it comes to trading it is much more significant to listen to the key policy makers.

The names you will want to look out for (at the time of writing) are Janet Yellen (Fed), Mario Draghi (ECB) and Mark Carney (BOE). You also need to be aware of which speakers have more impact than others. As explained above, when it comes to fundamental data and policy decisions the US will create the most movement in the financial markets. The Federal Open Market Committee (FOMC) and its members are the main drivers when it comes to this.

With the FOMC, pay attention to who is a voting member on policy; these people will have the most impact. Also pay attention to those who are not yet voting members but are scheduled to be and people who will potentially be elected on to the committee. This is sometimes the tiny amount of detail that can help you make the most of fundamental speaker comments while trading.

The 12 voting members of the FOMC are comprised of the seven members of the Federal Reserve Board and five of the 12 Federal Reserve Bank presidents. The New York Federal Reserve president is always a voting member of the committee. The tables below summarise the voting and non-voting members of the FOMC at the time of writing (the voting members change annually).

VOTING MEMBERS

Name	Position
Janet Yellen	Chair
Stanley Fischer	Vice-Chair

Name	Position
William Dudley	NY Fed President
Jerome Powell	Board Member
Daniel Tarullo	Board Member
Lael Brainard	Board Member
Charles Evans	Chicago Fed President
Jeffrey Lacker	Richmond Fed President
Dennis Lockhart	Atlanta Fed President
John Williams	San Francisco Fed President

NON-VOTING MEMBERS

Name	Position
James Bullard	St. Louis Fed President
Esther George	Kansas Fed President
Loretta Mester	Cleveland
Eric Rosengren	Boston Fed President
Christine Cumming	NY Fed Vice

As with other fundamental data, if central bank comments are new or unexpected by the market you will see a big reaction.

Trading example

This is an example of a press release from the former Fed Chairman Ben Bernanke on 18 September 2013 and the impact it had on the S&P 500. The press release said:

"To support continued progress toward maximum employment and price stability, the committee today reaffirmed its view that a highly accommodative stance of monetary policy will remain appropriate for a considerable time."

Chart 3 shows the S&P 500 from the H1 and D1 perspective after the market learnt of the Fed press release and Bernanke taking a dovish stance on quantitative easing (QE).

CHART 3: S&P 500 ON H1 AND D1

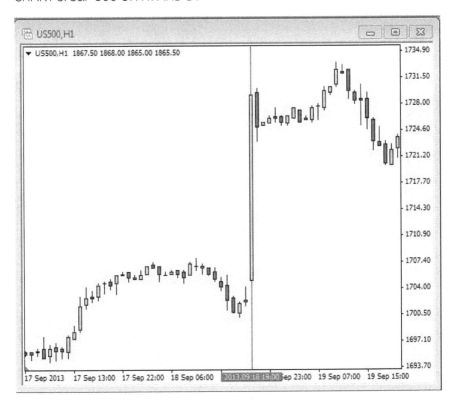

At this time the markets were still hungry for growth. Inflation was certainly not the main focus for traders, so this comment was a huge boost to the perception of short-term prosperity. This comment came well before the Fed began to taper QE and there had been many rumours and much speculation as to when the Fed would inevitably reduce QE.

The comment reiterated that the "highly accommodative" stance would remain appropriate for "a considerable time" and this was enough to see the S&P 500 rally over 240 pips in the space of an hour.

This is an example of an official Fed press release taking the markets by surprise. It was not the fact that the markets were not anticipating what was said, but more that it stopped the rumours and meant for the short term, at least, it was highly unlikely the Fed would taper QE. Therefore there was a rally into the already bullish indices.

As trading is so accessible these days, the ability to profit from volatility has increased dramatically. This in turn means that when you hear such a clear and tradable comment as in this instance there will be significant momentum brought into any strong directional move.

This is great if you are on the correct side of the trade. It also means, however, that what goes up will come down much more aggressively, as shown in the D1 chart.

In my experience, when fundamental comments are driving the market you have to be very cautious in picking a place where that momentum will stop. If you miss the initial central bank comment you may want to switch to the 15 minute charts and look for a continuation pattern. However, I'd suggest if you miss the initial wave then most of the time it is just worth staying out of the market altogether. It is sometimes possible to enter the market for the inevitable correction, but this will need both timing and patience.

Adding a technical indicator to the charts

Let's now look at the same charts but with a simple Fibonacci retracement added. Do not worry for now if you are unsure about Fibonacci – I will look at it in more detail in chapter 5.

The first chart – the hourly – is a very good example of how my 80/20 view of the markets works. If we take the hourly and apply the technical Fibonacci study from the high to the low, we can start to build a picture of how the new fundamental comments are affecting the demand for the S&P 500.

With Fibonacci, which is one of the technical tools I use most often, 80% of the time a directional overextended move will retrace to 50%. If this does not happen within a short time after the original directional move, the market will then go with the underlying trend and make a new high (or low).

As we are looking at the hourly (H1) chart (see Chart 4), I would say "a short time after" would be a maximum of one more hour.

CHART 4: S&P 500 H1 WITH FIBONACCI

This example is very useful because it shows the many aspects of Fibonacci and the interpretation needed:

1. The S&P did not attempt to retrace to the 50% and instead found support on the 23.6% retracement level and from there went on to make a new high.

2. After the initial spike there was fairly low volatility but the market remained above the 23.6% level and continued moving in the original direction until it made a new high once more. At this point the original resistance at 0.0%, the start of the original Fibonacci, became support.

3. Once the market had over-bought it retested the 0.0% level, where again it found support/resistance before it then targeted the lower Fibonacci retracement points.

4. The 23.6% and 38.2% acted as definite areas of interest before the market then retraced to the 50% level and below.

This simple principle gives us two interpretations but also two ways of trading this move for profit, both of which are after the event and after the institutional traders are out of the market. This means we have the option to make good trades based on fact and data, not just reacting to events.

Again, this technique only really applies to overextended moves. I class this as anything that trades more than 1.5 times the average trading range. In basic terms this is any directional candle with a fully body that extends in one direction significantly more than the previous candle bodies.

The daily chart

The daily (D1) chart (see Chart 5) is also interesting when applying the 80/20 rule. The same rules apply but the further you zoom out, or the higher time frame you look at, the longer things take to happen.

CHART 5: S&P 500 D1 WITH FIBONACCI

Notes:

1. As you would expect, the daily candle closes on the highs after the spike and fundamental comments drive up demand for the S&P.

2. A Fibonacci retracement is drawn from the high to the low of the day's trading and this encompasses all the trading activity and fundamental reaction. All of this is now priced into the market. On the open the next day, the price holds above the 38.2% level (rejecting the 50%) and goes on to make a new high.

3. The market does not then hold the new highs or make significant new lows. It closes on the 23.6% retracement level.

4. When the next day opens, the market trades lower from the previous day's close using the 23.6% as resistance and hitting the 50% retracement. It closes below 50%. This is the trigger for some significant downside potential. Again, as this is daily you have to be patient.

5. After a subsequent close below the 50%, there are then seven consecutive selling days, trading past the 100% retracement and finding support neatly on the 161.8% retracement. From here the market rebounded for a few days, but it couldn't even re-test back to the resistance at 100%, let alone the 50%, so the market then had no choice but to re-test the 161.8%. It then continued to break lower to the 261.8%.

The influence of the professionals

We've already seen that professional traders, banks and institutions all have the ability to move markets in any direction they choose prior to a scheduled data release and for a short period after. This can cause uncertainty and considerable doubt for the average trader. Remember that the markets are ruthless in stopping out weak traders.

Fundamental data is a red flag to professional traders. They know what you are likely to do based on the data. They know your average risk parameters and they know that you will doubt yourself.

As I have explained, once you understand the people within the markets you can start to understand your competition. You can then adjust your strategies to compensate for this factor.

The factor of time in fundamental moves

The longevity of the move is dictated by whether the news is expected or unexpected. You may hear the term "priced in" when trading and this means that the markets (especially the futures markets) have taken a view as to what will happen in the future with regards to fundamental data and set a market price accordingly.

The NFP we looked at above for gold is typical. The market was expecting a good figure, but not 113 points better. There was room to push gold significantly higher before letting it fall in accordance with what the data actually should do to gold. There was 45 minutes of pain, which is a tremendous amount of time in intraday trading, before the single 15 minutes of pleasure and profit-taking.

This happens in most markets, from bonds to oil. If anything unexpected hits the markets then this view may be either enhanced or detracted from, leading to an overextended move as traders readjust their positions accordingly. Anything that happens that is exceptional and completely unexpected by the markets, like a terror attack, once again levels the playing field. Any traders basing their decisions on that news will all be trading at the same time and with the same information.

When markets move around new data and news it is important to remember that there may be existing sentiment. This is the 20% I refer to and may be the underlying trend. If this new information contradicts the current sentiment, traders may use this as a short-term measure to trade against that trend to make money.

* * *

I am a huge believer in the 80/20 rule. I strongly maintain that all traders need to be aware of the fundamental impact news will have on their technical trading and analysis. You simply can't be a consistent day trader if you do not have a balance of the two.

On that note, let's move on to look at the technical aspect in more detail.

CHAPTER 5.
My 80/20 Rule – Overview of 80% Technical

SOME TYPES OF TECHNICAL ANALYSIS – CANDLESTICKS FOR example – have been around for centuries, but I am not going to go too far back in time. For what is relevant in today's markets, we only have to go back to the days of the trading pits and live floors.

At that time, traders didn't need to know too much about the technical analysis of markets. Being in an open outcry pit they could hear and feel the market sentiment all around them. They could physically see the order flow and individuals buying and selling contracts. With some basic understanding of current market value and basic key levels, they could trade very successfully.

Once the live floors closed and the majority of traders moved on to trading screens, all this changed. There was no noise, no orders or traders to physically see, just rows of screens. All types of traders and personalities were merged together and obscured.

A different type of trader was created. It was out with the old pit-style trader and in with the new technical trader. This is why 80% of modern intraday trading is based on technical analysis.

Having worked on, and managed, many trading floors over the years, I would say they are now actually fairly sterile, quiet, and well, office-like. Traders need to concentrate on multiple screens, assimilating massive amounts of market data and studying the 80% rule of technical analysis.

When the noise went, so did a lot of the emotion and drama. Not all the drama I may add – I have seen people throw their computer mice across the room, smashing them against the wall. Traders spit at their screens and hit them, and there has also been the odd punch up along the way too. On the whole, however, the trading floors of today are nothing like the live floors of the past. Technical analysis of charts is now the order of the day.

In this chapter I am going to explain how I use technical analysis. The important topics are:

1. The self-fulfilling prophecy

2. Markets have a memory

3. Candlesticks – why we use them, what to look for

4. Time frames and support and resistance

5. Indicators and oscillators

6. Gaps

7. Fibonacci and the significance of overextended markets

1. The self-fulfilling prophecy

There is a common belief about technical analysis being self-fulfilling. If the majority of market participants look at a certain indicator, trend or technical aspect, then it's more likely to come true.

What's most interesting about this is that people assume technical analysis will hold conclusive answers about the way markets are likely to behave. If you buy into the self-fulfilling idea then you believe that something technical has to hold some significance at some point. You will eventually probably be right. It doesn't necessarily mean, however, that it will happen when you think it will, or that you will make money out of it.

Another interesting point is that if we are all looking for the same answers from the same technical analysis, does this not leave us open to manipulation? If the mass of traders are looking at technical analysis, they will be following the well-

known rules of the patterns. Other traders will know this and can then use it to their advantage. I see it happen every day in the markets.

Chart 6 provides a simple demonstration using the RSI indicator with GBP/ USD. Retail traders would have been selling at 70 on the RSI chart (this is the common overbought level) so the professional traders would have pushed the market higher. Then the market subsequently went down as everyone expected. Retail traders would have been short squeezed or stopped out before the expected movement down materialised.

CHART 6: GBP/USD WITH RSI

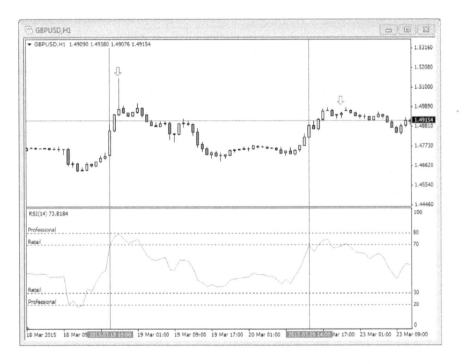

Why does this happen? It's all to do with timing.

When you trade intraday you may be looking at a 5 minute candle or a 15 minute candle. A lot can happen in that short space of time and things can start to look very different very quickly, especially when you are on the wrong side of the market. This is where the self-fulfilling prophecy works best for me.

If we are reaching a key technical level in a market then often the opposite of what you believe to be true can happen in the short term before the inevitability of the self-fulfilling prophecy kicks in.

Let's look at an example of the DAX.

Example: DAX

The market closed strongly at the end of 2013 and opened strongly into 2014. There was every likelihood for the DAX to trade higher and go on to target the 10,000 level.

Why 10,000?

This is a round number, which is a psychological target for traders. If the market has to make new highs not traded before then a round number like this is a point of attraction. The fundamentals within the global economy were relatively sound and by 21 January 2014 the market was less than 210 pips away from this significant level – which is a range easily achievable in a single day's trading.

The markets had rallied into the New Year and all the technical key support levels remained intact, so it was simply a matter of time before the DAX fulfilled the market's bullish sentiment and made new highs.

Chart 7 shows the DAX's move towards the psychological round number target of 10,000.

CHART 7: DAX

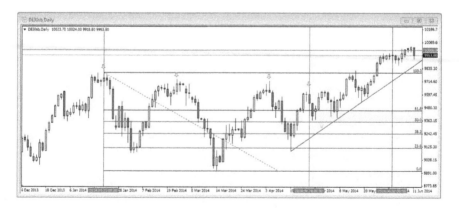

As you can see, the markets are not as clear cut or accommodating as we might hope. Just because 10,000 is a key technical and psychological level, it does not mean the market will trade straight there. Indeed, it did not.

Although the tops were tantalisingly close on a few occasions and the majority of market participants would have been expecting new highs, in the short term the DAX did the opposite! From the high point on 21 January of 9794.30 (marked by the vertical line) there was an aggressive sell off for the next week, targeting 9000.

This is where the judgment calls and trading strategy come into their own:

- For the **longer-term trader**, holding out for the highs, is this really the market condition for a correction?

- For the **short-term intraday** trader, is this a time to sell high and follow profit takers?

This is why it is so important to have a clear trading style and plan. You can find yourself caught up in whipsaw action and lose money on trades which are only correct depending on the time frame and trade type you adopt.

On the daily charts from here the DAX made three attempts to get to 10,000. All three of these contained an indecision candle and led to the market moving lower. It was not until May that the market traded consistently above 9345, the 50% retracement levels for the January highs, and we could draw in a good support line giving the market room to the upside.

Once again, the only real psychological and technical target to aim for at this point is the 10,000 mark.

Longer-term trader

For the longer-term trader who holds overnight positions, it would now be easier to buy low and use the diagonal trend as support with 10,000 as a target. Since the market never broke or closed below this trend line, the self-fulfilling nature of the strong uptrend – and the fact that the 10,000 level is such a clear target – meant this was a relatively simple trade.

All you had to do was position yourself correctly and wait for the uptrend to gather momentum and return. The actual high point of this move was 9988.80 before the market lost momentum. For any longer-term trader there would have been the temptation to bank a profit early. After this high was hit there were two more daily closes before the 10,000 mark was eventually hit.

Intraday trader

An intraday trader would have to identify the relative low point of the day and try to catch the momentum that would drive the market up towards 10,000. This is when intraday trading has significant benefits. The trade setup and the trend have been identified on the daily charts and as intraday traders we could use that framework to zoom in and pick an opportunity from the more sensitive H1 (hourly) time frame.

From the hourly perspective we could see that although the market was in a downtrend channel, the lows of the highlighted candles were rejected. When H1 candles leave a significant wick in the opposite direction of the trend this always highlights that a shift in sentiment is due.

The market then moved into a pennant formation, where it began to find support and move higher. The very last attempt for an H1 candle to close lower was rejected (indicated by the arrow) and then the market broke and closed outside the resistance of the trend channel. From this point it took only one further hourly candle to hit the 10,000 mark (see Chart 8).

CHART 8: DAX H1

This shows why it is good practice to look at the charts on different time scales. It is what I call "all time frame trading."

A good way of viewing the markets is to have a D1 chart, H1 chart and M15 chart of the same product side by side on your charting setup. You can then pick up points of interest and make judgement calls on how the market may move intraday, just like the example in FAQ 2 from chapter 1.

2. Markets have a memory

One of the most commonly used technical analysis tools is support and resistance. This needs very little interpretation: when buyers outstrip sellers the market moves towards resistance, and vice versa. I tend to regard support and resistance as points of interest, or BOB (break or bounce) levels.

This means I don't have to give myself a predetermined bias to buy or sell. It's just something that is worth looking at as the price approaches these levels.

First we have to identify how the markets are behaving. Markets within a range will treat support and resistance very differently to markets that are trending and breaking out.

Example: WTI

Commodities tend to be fairly sensitive to fundamental data and news events. Here is a good example of taking a basic channel pattern and using the principle that the market has a memory, using WTI crude oil.

Chart 9 shows a typical example of a trend channel drawn on the M15 chart. The market established support and then trended upwards until a technical break down.

This is not a textbook example of a trend channel, but you have to consider that if it looks like a trend channel and behaves like a trend channel, then it probably is a trend channel (the self-fulfilling nature of technical analysis once again). I have found over the years that simple, clear technical analysis just works.

I have also plotted other market memory points of interest, or where the market should continue to break or eventually bounce up from the down move. These were drawn using previous points of interest from further back in the chart.

CHART 9: WTI CRUDE OIL M15

You have to go quite far back in the chart to get some 15m lower levels, but 103.56, 103.37 and 103.10 act as points of interest on this 15 minute view.

If we are doing our technical analysis correctly we should know what happened in the past to try and predict the future. Chart 10 is an M15 view of the past, showing what we know has happened.

CHART 10: WTI CRUDE OIL M15

Looking back in the chart we can identify previous points of attraction when the market was trending up. We can then use these levels as potential support levels or points of attraction as the market breaks down.

It is always fairly easy to show a chart like this and prove any theory. This is why I advise people to look at the daily, hourly and 15 minute charts on a regular basis to get a balanced view between the relative short-term and long-term views for intraday trading.

Where did WTI go on to trade in 2014? The answer is well below $100 – at the time of writing the price is $51 a barrel.

The longer time frames, in this case M1, will always be significant for traders working with smaller time frames. The next example, Chart 11, is an M1 chart of EUR/USD. It shows the market consistently making lower highs. These M1 levels are very important for intraday traders.

CHART 11: EUR/USD M1

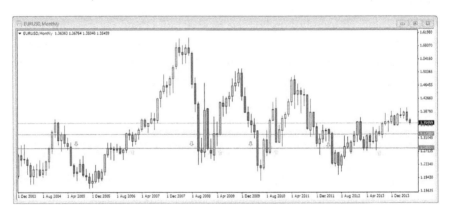

The more action you see around a particular point of interest, the more chance it will have relevance in the future. I look specifically for consecutive opens and closes around these lines and also when they have acted as turning points to reverse the trend and to carry on trading higher or lower.

Look for obvious and well-known patterns

Remember the self-fulfilling prophecy. Double bottoms and tops are always of interest to traders, and so are head and shoulders patterns. You can go overboard trying to pick out the perfect levels and chart patterns. If you plot your support and resistance lines and they look significant and have some of the characteristics I have mentioned above you will not go far wrong.

Don't over complicate support and resistance

If it looks right it usually is. You might think, "Well, that is all obvious and I already knew that's how to plot support and resistance." You would be surprised how many people do not plot support and resistance like this.

For a start, I am using candlesticks; this is vitally important when getting levels. You can use bars but they do not hold the same self-fulfilling nature that candles do. Candles have their own language, with a set of individual and multiple formation interpretations.

When it comes to technical trading, we need to build upon the tried and tested approaches. The self-fulfilling prophecy of technical analysis goes hand in hand with the fact that previous points of attraction hold relevance to traders in the future.

3. Candlesticks – why we use them, what to look for

There are fads and cycles in technical analysis. In the early days I was taught about the bell curve and market profile. We then progressed to bars. I remember one of my early mentors telling me about inside bars as if the information was equivalent to a set of nuclear launch codes – the most precious information ever passed on.

For me, candlestick charts hold very clear advantages over bar charts; they are the best way of viewing a chart. What I like about candles is that they are very visual. You can get a quick idea from the candle body as to the direction, strength and volume within a market. However, useful though they are, remember you have to combine individual candle patterns and clusters of patterns with your other technical analysis tools.

When using candlesticks I often get asked how I plot my trend lines. Do I use high/low or open/close? So here's a Ruff tip:

RUFF TIP

In my technical analysis I find that diagonal **trend lines** work best from the highs and lows, and straight lines of **support** work best with corresponding opens/closes.

Example: EUR/USD

Chart 12 shows M1 charts with the same price action in EUR/USD variously displayed in candles and bars.

In the candlestick chart we can see a single hammer formation. At the bottom of a trend this is a very strong reversal candle.

CHART 12: EUR/USD M1

Looking at the candlestick chart, once the market broke the level 1.28054, the EUR/USD rallied and then subsequently closed at the next significant point of interest: 1.32188. We could have identified this from what happened previously in the chart. This is not as easy to identify on the bar chart.

The point of technical analysis is that you have to use all the tools at your disposal. For key technical levels to be useful in the market they have to not only look right but also need to have been plotted by other traders. The action areas that I refer to are going to give you a much better set of levels than always plotting absolute highs and lows of prices traded.

Using candlesticks

The key to using candlesticks in your trading is to know what purpose you are using them for. We can split this into two parts:

1. Evaluation

2. Indication

1. Evaluation

I use hourly candles to spot the current trend and then identify from the candles how this movement is made up. The trend is easy – you don't need candles to tell you this – but the way each individual candle closes will give you an indication of how strong the underlying trend is.

Chart 13 is an H1 of EUR/JPY. After the downtrend we can see that there was then a series of consecutive higher lows.

For the purposes of the example, let's pretend we can't see to the right-hand side of the line in the chart. This is not a perfect scenario, or even a chart that ideally illustrates my principles; it's just a real-world trading example that shows the type of setup I look for.

1. I start without any technical analysis on the chart and look for a combination of large bodies or large wicks that may indicate there will be a change in the underlying trend.

2. We can see a clear downtrend to the left of the chart, with a mixture of candle types. Once the market consolidates with a number of indecision candles, it then drops down further (marked with an arrow). This is where I would have gained an initial interest in this particular market. The next candle exhibits a large wick but closes up, which indicates that there is not enough momentum to carry the market lower – the candle closes with little real directional bias.

3. The next candle (marked with another arrow) opens around the previous close and then moves higher. This evaluation tells me that there is a potential change in the underlying downtrend.

CHART 13: EUR/JPY H1

As I have previously mentioned, the market will often do the opposite in the short term of what you think, before then fulfilling your trade call. This is why I say this is the *evaluation* stage.

From this point, I would then use the candles and other tools to support my potential trade call. I look for a combination of an individual candle or candlesticks, together with my technical analysis, that will allow me to put on a good trade.

2. Indication

Trading from the H1 time frame has always given me enough time to evaluate the situation based on what has happened in the past. I then have the chance to predict what could happen in the future based on that view. With the H1 charts, you have to remember that the full move will take time to materialise and that you have to be patient in order to get the correct entry and potential exit.

Still referring the chart above:

1. The first upwards arrow and the up move from that point still fall into my evaluation criteria. This is not enough to make me get into the trade.

2. I'm looking for a combination of factors that give me a trade call resulting from the evaluation. Once again, as this is an H1 analysis it means that the trade call I want may not happen for some time.

Chart 14 shows what takes place after the vertical line.

CHART 14: EUR/JPY H1

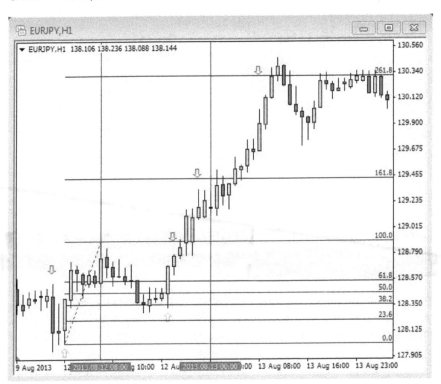

Notes:

1. From the initial upwards arrow, the market went on to make a significant high where the first vertical line is drawn. In the short term this was the overall high before the market then dropped off.

2. After the initial downwards arrow and the sell off, I would class the first upwards arrow to the top of the candle on the vertical line as a significant directional up move. I state in my Fibonacci rules that 80% of the time, a strong directional move will retrace to the 50% retracement point.

3. In this example the market did just that. It not only retraced to the 50%, but broke to the 38.2%.

RUFF TIP

I have drawn the Fibonacci retracement from the high to the low. This means the retracement numbers are the opposite way around. I will explain why I did this in the Fibonacci section, but in a nutshell I am expecting a short-term reversal so I want to know in relation to the 50% retracement point (which will not move) where the other expansion levels (161.8%, 261.8% and 423.6%) will be for future reference.

---

4. The fact that the market retraced to the 50% point is reassuring, as it proves my Fibonacci theory. The fact that it stalled at this point and did not retrace 100% of the move is even better, as it gives credibility to the theory the market may have reversed the initial downtrend and was continuing the new bull trend we have identified in our analysis.

5. When the market found support on the 38.2% retracement point and traded higher, it was when the market opened on the 50% point (second upwards arrow) that we had an indication the market would now make a full reversal of the downtrend and a new high.

6. Within two more hourly candles the market traded to the 100% level and the high point the Fibonacci retracement level was drawn from.

Remembering the self-fulfilling prophecy and the fact the market has a memory, I look for the last significant point of resistance to be support within the market. The last point of resistance was where we drew our Fibonacci from, the 100%. This then exhibited two up candles opening on this price, with two supporting wicks making a double bottom at 123.867 (thumbs up symbol in Chart 15). This is where I would buy the EUR/JPY.

After the evaluation and the indication it is now time to trade the market. This is the entry point for the continuation trade in the EUR/JPY.

CHART 15: EUR/JPY H1

You may think that this point is too late, or not an optimal entry point, but in my experience trying to get in at the exact point the market turns is very difficult. I want to trade with the new trend and ride on the back of the new momentum.

Review

1. More technical analysis can be added to the chart in the form of RSI (see chart above). This will give me a good visual aid for following the market up. Although the RSI is considered overbought at 70, if this level acts as support then we will see much more momentum come into the market. As this is a reversal of a downtrend this will help a long position gain even more traction.

2. The double bottom wicks and the two candles opening on the 100% of resistance that is now acting as support is a good confirming indicator. The large up candle bodies support the reversal and from the second upwards arrow there are seven buying candles before an indecision candle. This candle does nothing to send the market back into the range or start a sell off, so this indicates that more upside momentum is likely.

3. The horizontal lines represent the overextension levels 161.8%, 261.8% and potentially 423.6% that I have identified as potential exit points. I explained how I drew the Fibonacci levels in the opposite way to normal so I could get the retracement points relative to the 50% to the upside. These retracement points now act as points of attraction in relation to where the market found support.

Formations and time frames

There are certain candlestick formations that work well on specific time frames. Once we are familiar with this we can then see how two or more candles can form much more powerful signals.

For intraday trading I still maintain the hourly charts hold some of the best signals. But you can also use the daily charts to get an idea of what may happen soon. You will generally be looking for a reversal or continuation of the current trend.

Doji

The doji is one of the best candle formations for this. It is simple to spot and appears frequently enough to be of use, but not so frequently it is over-traded and constantly discounted.

A doji is identified by having no, or very little, candle body. The wicks are generally short, but this is not always the case. This is where a trader's interpretation comes into play. You are looking for indecision in the market – a turning point.

Example

Chart 16 provides an example of a doji towards the low of an increasingly strong down move in GBP/USD on a D1 chart.

CHART 16: GBP/USD D1

In this example there is no candle body and the fact that the wicks are the same length means it is easy to identify this as a doji. As the market is making lower highs (highlighted by the boxes I have drawn on the chart), when the doji is formed (the thumbs up symbol) this means that the downtrend should prevail and that the market should move lower. We then see four days of selling action that could be used for intraday trades.

We have seen how the doji on the daily chart indicates a good continuation of a trend, and can lead to a good bias for shorter-term trades. This is a good way to introduce yourself to using the trend and candlesticks to help form an opinion and trade call.

RUFF TIP

Do not fall into the trap of thinking that candles are now always the perfect answer to trading charts. Candles have to be used as just part of your technical strategy – you need a combination of indicators such as Fibonacci, Bollinger Bands or RSI to help make your call.

Gaps

Some of the best candlestick formations revolve around gaps. Gaps, both intraday and overnight, indicate something significant has hit the market. This can generally be attributed to new fundamental data being released, or sometimes it's due to technical stops.

Example

This example is on the hourly chart of USD/CHF and shows how a short-term bias can be formed and then continued (see Chart 17). I refer to this style of formation as an *island pattern*. These patterns are identified by two gaps originating from when the start of the island forms, and a clear rejection of that gap being closed, to a secondary gap leaving the island of candles separated from the new movement in the chart. Both gaps support the direction of the down move.

Notes:

1. Once the gap found a low on the first candle (upward arrow) the start of the island was formed. The market then trended between the horizontal lines, which formed the low and high of the island formation.

2. The market attempted to close the gap to the upside but at the first downward arrow the market indicated that the final attempt to close the initial gap had been rejected. From the initial gap to the attempted close was a significant passage of time in intraday trading, so the fact that the down gap was still in play meant that the market would look to test the previous key point of support before re-testing the gap.

3. Once the lowest point traded after the gap was broken (horizontal line) the market closed on the low of the hourly candle that broke it.

4. The next hourly candle then opened with another down gap, leaving the cluster – or formation of candlesticks – on their own as an island.

5. This then triggered a huge selling candle and the market continued to trade downwards.

CHART 17: USD/CHF H1

As with all the candle patterns I have demonstrated, the element of time is a very important factor.

I will cover gaps in more detail in their own section later in this chapter.

4. Time frames and support and resistance

Short-term traders can fall into the trap of looking at tick or minute data, thinking this gives them the best view of what will happen next. Looking at a one minute chart for example – the lowest time frame I use for technical non-data trades – within 15 minutes you will get 15 potential signals. For a chart spanning one hour, which is what I focus on, you'll of course get 60 potential signals with minute data.

So if you are an intraday trader and basing a trade on 15 or 60 signals at a time, what are your chances of success?

My view is, why not zoom out to the 15m or hourly charts and get four signals over one hour or even just one better quality hourly signal? Remember that both these time frames are made up of the same minute data. For longer-term trading you may want to use daily closes or opens for your areas of interest and trade entries.

You will want to look at points of attraction from the bigger picture and the higher time frame that you are entering the trade from.

Example 1: EUR/USD monthly, weekly and daily

Chart 18 shows two trade setups in EUR/USD, one for a longer-term position trade and one for intraday. The aim is to achieve a view on what the market has done in the past and what it may do in the future.

My point is to show you how you can switch the time frames to suit your needs and also that when you view different time frame data you are essentially looking at the same thing.

By zooming out to the monthly time frame you can see the bigger picture. This is where you want to build up your ideas of where the market has traded before and where the significant points of interest were. You can then determine where the market may go to in the future.

As ever, my initial analysis is based on Fibonacci and the tried and tested support and resistance lines.

CHART 18: EUR/USD

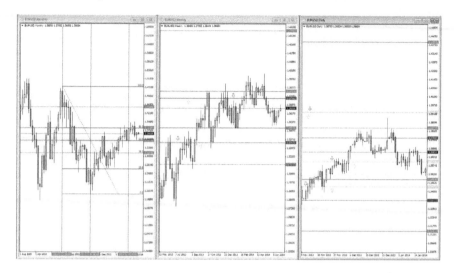

RUFF TIP

Do not be tempted to go too far back in the charts. Bear in mind that technical data is also made up of fundamentals. If you go too far back in time, you may be comparing current sentiment with a market that was focusing on very different factors.

1. When looking at the monthly chart of EUR/USD we see that from mid-2011 the market peaked and there was a clear reversal in the demand for the euro. The market then sold off for over a year. I would call this a significant direction move. Remember the basic rule: 80% of the time a strong directional move will retrace to the 50% Fibonacci retracement level.

2. By early 2014 the market had reached 1.34836. We can use this as a point of reference and use the other key Fibonacci levels (61.8% and 38.2%) as points of significant attraction in future trading.

3. On the monthly chart I would also plot any other points of interest that I thought could be relevant in the future. So in this case, it looks like there was some significant closing action around the 1.43888 level.

Transferring the points of interest to shorter time frame charts

I then transfer these monthly levels to the other time frame charts from which I make my trades.

In this case, as we are looking for the longer-term trade, I'm using the weekly and the daily charts. I pick out significant points of weekly interest in terms of support and resistance by looking at the highs, lows, opens and closes. Then I will take all this data and do the same with the daily chart.

It all seems fairly laborious, but I produced the above charts manually in ten minutes. Once you have taken your monthly view down to the daily charts and filled in the time frame gaps with support and resistance, you will now have a much clearer idea of where the markets will move to; you have a structured framework of meaningful support and resistance.

Chart 19 is an example of the D1 EUR/USD with all the M1, W1 and D1 points of interest drawn on.

From this point you can then trade the daily opens and closes with a view to where the most logical point of support and resistance will be found. You can then also use your basic trend lines and add indicators, like RSI, to be able to make clearer, more informed trade calls.

I find that the support and resistance lines are the only way to get a clear idea of what the market may do based on what it has already done. What I find reassuring about the monthly and weekly Fibonacci levels is that they are clear for anyone to see and therefore trade. There is little to no interpretation required between 2011 and mid-2012. This is the self-fulfilling nature of technical analysis again.

What is also useful when charting in this way is that it is not only the longer-term trader that can benefit from this style of technical analysis. The levels you generate are also of use to short-term intraday traders. You can basically take these levels and apply then to your hourly and 15 minute charts – after all, it's all part of the same picture.

CHART 19: EUR/USD D1

Let's look at an example.

Example 1: EUR/USD hourly

I try to find out what is of interest from the hourly movement and try to build a view around that. This may lead to a point of interest for trade entries.

I would take a significant hourly Fibonacci from a key low to a key high to understand what the relatively short-term trading is telling me. I would also include the RSI. Using the 50% Fibonacci as an hourly pivot we can then see how the intraday traders will use the higher time frame levels of support and resistance as possible targets.

Chart 20 shows EUR/USD on the H1 chart after a significant move up. We are looking for the key 50% retracement.

CHART 20: EUR/USD H1

Chart 21 shows EUR/USD on the H1 chart after a 50% retracement level. We can see the market used the 50% as a pivot and broke lower beyond this point.

CHART 21: EUR/USD H1

Notes:

1. Once the 38.2% Fibonacci retracement line acted as support and then resistance on the way down, the 50% retracement level became the major attraction point.

2. The market then uses the daily (marked on Chart 21) as another point of support/resistance before then breaking down to test the 100% level, which was the start of the move up.

3. All the time, the hourly RSI is supporting the direction of the move.

This is how you can use all the higher time frames and points of attraction to trade intraday.

5. Indicators and oscillators

Traders use indicators to help them make decisions based on chart patterns; they are another form of confirmation. They are calculations that help to verify the quality of a chart pattern or setup and form a decision on a buy or sell.

They do not take into account fundamental events, but traders will use them in combination with other fundamental and technical tools to give a balanced approach to making trade calls.

Indicators are generally split into:

1. **Leading indicators**, which try to predict price movement.

2. **Lagging indicators**, which are seen more as confirming indicators as they follow existing price movements.

In practice all indicators are based on historic data so there is always an element of lag. This is why you need to understand the underlying market movement, and if the market is ranging or strongly trending, as different indicators will be more or less useful depending on the trading conditions.

Indicators that use a range (usually between 0-100 or 0-1) are referred to as *oscillators*. The basic premise is that they give an idea of whether the underlying market is, say, overbought (0) or oversold (100). There are significant ranges for most of the oscillators. For instance, RSI is considered overbought at 30 and oversold at 70. These are the settings I have used on the chart examples in this book, as they are what I look for.

Indicators that are not range-bound use parameters such as time or data periods to display a line or some sort of graphical representation on the chart. As I always use a combination of both types – oscillators and non-oscillators – I will just refer to indicators.

These are the indicators I like to use on hourly charts:

1. Relative strength index (RSI)

2. DeMark Indicator (DeM)

3. Bollinger Bands

I will now look at these in turn.

1. Relative strength index (RSI)

The RSI indicator ranges between 0-100, so it's an oscillator. It measures the speed and change of price movement. It was developed by J. Welles Wilder.

With this indicator, oversold territory is often assumed to be below 30, overbought above 70, and with the potential for divergence around the 50 mark.

Chart 22 shows an example of an H1 chart of EUR/USD going from overbought (70) to oversold (30) and the subsequent market direction.

CHART 22: EUR/USD H1

The 14 period RSI is quite typical when setting up your indicators. I generally use the 14 day for RSI, but as you'll see I use 20 periods for Bollinger Bands. The lower the number of periods you use, the more likely you will see whipsaws between overbought and oversold. The more periods you use, the smoother the curve and the less frequently you will hit the upper and lower extremes.

The period you use is up to you. I would always start with an indicator's default settings, as this will mean you are using the same settings as most other traders (the good old self-fulfilling prophecy again).

The RSI should be used to support your view of the trend. It can also help you determine where the markets are overextended, so overbought on the high side and oversold on the low side.

How to find overbought and oversold territories

I have previously explained how you get a framework with support and resistance levels. You should use the RSI to catch tops and bottoms using the oversold (30) and overbought (70) industry standards.

Chart 23 is an H1 for EUR/USD. The RSI hits the oversold (30) mark. We are looking to identify a bottom and key support levels to confirm the bounce.

CHART 23: EUR/USD H1

Notes:

1. The large vertical line shows the point where the market hit the lower trend line and the RSI was at 31.

2. These are two confirming indicators that could mean a bounce higher is the technical trade.

3. From the low of the trend line there was a good entry point. The 38.2% Fibonacci line, which is marked on the chart, provides a good potential exit point.

4. For good measure, the down candle on the large vertical line looks overextended in relation to the rest of the market.

5. I took the Fibonacci from the low to the high of this candle to get the 50% (remember, 80% of the time an overextended move retraces to 50%), so 1.36556 was also a very good potential intraday exit point.

2. DeMark Indicator (DeM)

I like to use the DeMark in conjunction with RSI. As it is an oscillator it uses the same parameters as RSI but between 0-1, so 0.3 and 0.7 indicate oversold and overbought respectively.

I use DeM more as a potential bear and bull reversal indicator, rather than for overbought or oversold territories. I find this gives me a better mental trigger of what to expect. I also keep the 14 period, but expand my parameters to 0.2 and 0.8 for the extremes of the reversal.

Chart 24 is an H1 of AUD/NZD, showing the DeM highs and lows and subsequent change in market direction.

I have found that adjusting DeM to 0.2 and 0.8 offers better turning points and triggers for trade confirmations. Where the curves of RSI are a little smoother in getting to the extremes, DeM is a lot clearer on rejections and offers a sharper movement line.

I generally trade at the potential extremes of the markets, so I don't tend to use the RSI or DeM for divergence, just for a buy/sell or a potential confirmation of trend direction. This is, of course, something you could look at: taking the midpoint of RSI and DeM and trying to identify possible breakouts or trend continuation.

CHART 24: AUD/NZD H1

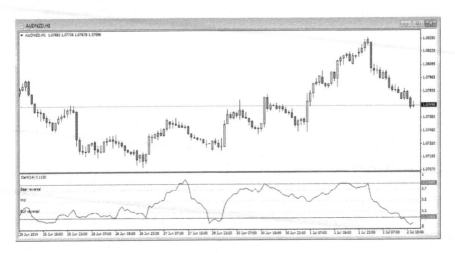

Combining indicators

As I feel more comfortable selling the extremes of the markets, I like to use RSI and DeM to get an idea of when the markets are due a turn. I have found that doing this with the individual hourly candle formations has been a good way of charting and getting consistent calls.

Chart 25 is an H1 for AUD/NZD showing the correlation between DeM and RSI.

This is a nice way to get extra confirmation from your indicators and try to combat any short-term possible manipulation in the market. It is a lot easier to spot a potentially overbought or oversold RSI area with a comforting DeM reversal signal backing it up.

CHART 25: AUD/NZD H1

3. Bollinger Bands

Bollinger Bands are a very simple concept and like most things, the simplest solutions are usually the best ones.

Bollinger Bands are two lines (an upper and lower) that are two standard deviations around a moving average (MA). The time period for the moving average can be adjusted; it is usually 20, which is fine. You can use Bollinger Bands with different types of moving average (e.g. exponential), but I would recommend sticking to a simple MA.

I have encountered very little technical analysis that does not refer to MAs at some point. With Bollinger Bands you get the MA information, plus two other boundaries where the market will find support and resistance.

The other reason I like Bollinger Bands is that when they are combined with tools like Fibonacci, RSI or DeM, they provide some of the most consistent signals I have encountered.

Unlike RSI and DeM, the bands do not use a scale, so it is not classed as an oscillator. This can lead to people being confused about how to interpret them. Having said that, you can certainly class the upper and lower bands as overbought and oversold in terms of support and resistance in the time frame you are using.

I would only use Bollinger Bands on hourly charts and higher. There is a rare occasion when I will look at them on the 15 minute chart if I am looking for a precise entry, but this is very infrequent.

Bollinger Bands for market extremes

I use the Bollinger Bands at the extremes of the market as this is where I feel I get the most value. The markets do not like to trade outside the upper and lower Bollinger Bands for any sustained length of time, so this is where I tend to focus my attention.

It is also possible to use the midpoint as a significant point of interest and use the upper or lower bands as a target. Whether you can do this depends on whether the market is trending or ranging (see below) and what your view on the market is.

If you look at any market on an hourly view you will see Bollinger Bands and candles exhibit the same pattern time and time again: the market will close outside the upper or lower band, consolidate and then re-target the midpoint.

When markets close outside the Bollinger Bands one of two things will usually happen:

1. There will be an exaggerated directional move away from the upper or lower band and the market will exhibit a breakout trending movement.

2. You will see a period of consolidation and the market will then gradually look to get back to the midpoint (or MA) and then the opposite Bollinger band.

When charting with Bollinger Bands it is especially important to know if the market is exhibiting ranging or trending characteristics. In this way you can treat the bands with a view to being support and resistance or possible breakout points. This means thinking of the 80/20 rule and making sure you have priced in the fundamentals and also focusing on the candle bodies to establish potential volatility. The market characteristics will not only determine how the Bollinger Bands behave but also how to trade using them.

RUFF TIP

I refer to most technical levels as 'points of interest' as they will only act as support or resistance depending on the way the market is trading. A support level in a heavily trending, bearish market is more likely to be a point to break than to bounce from, so should not actually be viewed as support at all.

Looking at Bollinger Bands can often lead you into a false sense of security as they appear to provide a good indication of how the markets have functioned in terms of significant support and resistance. Do not fall into this trap – it is important to use Bollinger Bands as part of a strategy and not just as a single indicator to trade from.

Textbook Bollinger band explanations say that bands which are close together indicate low volatility and when bands are far apart there is high volatility. This is the case, however as the Bollinger Bands are based on moving averages (usually the 20 period) they always lag to a degree. The actual candle bodies will tell us when the market is currently volatile.

Let's look at an example.

Example: USD/CHF

Chart 26 is an H1 of USD/CHF. You can see that closes outside of the upper or lower bands lead back to the midpoint.

CHART 26: USD/CHF H1

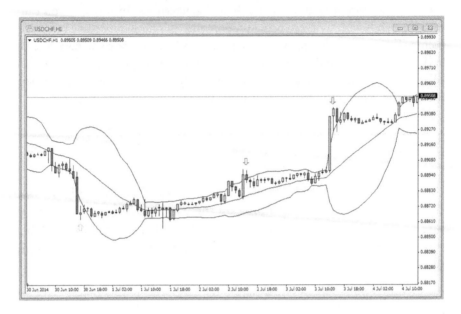

Notes:

1. The first upward arrow shows the market breaking the lower band on an aggressive downward move.

2. The market then closed two further candles outside the lower band, indicating consolidation, and then the market limped back to the moving average after many hours.

We could interpret this as a good buying opportunity. However, this would be with the benefit of hindsight. While the Bollinger Bands were forming on the hourly chart this would not have been so clear.

Chart 27 shows an H1 of USD/CHF in a downtrend. You can see how the upper band offers resistance points.

CHART 27: USD/CHF H1

If we go back to basics we see that between the vertical lines the market is actually finding increasing resistance:

1. The upper band is acting as strong resistance, as is the MA.

2. We can pick out candle highs and lows to form a descending trend channel.

3. The market was moving lower and the Bollinger Bands were close together (indicating low volatility).

The key is to remember that the overall trend we have identified is down. We are looking for a potential trigger for the volatility to return and for the Bollinger band to widen.

Confirming the downtrend

In essence, we are not using the Bollinger Bands as a breakout point, we are using them to confirm the downtrend.

1. The candle bodies are relatively small. We are looking for the consolidating, close together Bollinger Bands to expand and create a further continuation of the overall trend.

2. The trigger is indicated by the box in Chart 28. We have an individual hammer followed by an engulfing candle. Although this is not 100% engulfing, in this case it is close enough (in technical analysis you need some interpretation).

3. This area indicates that there is a battle between the bulls and bears. If the market wanted to break the downtrend and go back up, technically it could have from this point.

4. The size and close of the next down candle indicates to me the downtrend is still very much in play.

Chart 28 shows an H1 of USD/CHF, using the Bollinger band resistance and DeM to confirm a downtrend.

The market then continued to close below the MA and the volatility picked up. This example shows why the H1 chart is good for seeing how the market will unfold, but bear in mind you may have needed to view the same chart on the M15 time frame to get the best intraday trading wins.

CHART 28: USD/CHF H1

6. Gaps

As discussed earlier in relation to candlestick formations, gaps appear in the markets as a result of a sudden significant shift in supply and demand. This means the market moves in one direction with orders being pulled and traders aggressively buying or selling at the next available price, forming a gap. These gaps form some of the most powerful technical candlestick formations, reversal and continuation trend patterns; their very occurrence brings traders into the market.

Gaps that appear on daily charts are generally a result of overnight news, so a gap in the FTSE on the open could be due to events that happened in the US or Asia while the FTSE was closed. The candlestick formations that are generated from these gaps on the higher time frames generally indicate potential continuation or reversal patterns.

Since you see these on the daily charts and above, the formations are good to trade from the hourly perspective. These types of technical formations resulting from gaps act as a trigger for what can happen next in the markets.

You can, of course, look at the hourly and 15 minute time frames, and even shorter, when you see intraday gaps. You can see small intraday gaps when strong directional moves happen.

I personally like to use a gap as an indicator for what will happen next. I try to get an idea of why the gap formed and, more importantly, what the market intends to do with it. And, I should say, a gap will only be a part of an overall trade strategy.

A gap usually occurs between two candles but you can get a series of gaps, which illustrates the importance of formations and also the element of time when considering trading gaps. I choose the next example to demonstrate that – be it a fundamentally driven gap or technically triggered stop – there are a few basic rules that come into play.

Example

In Chart 29 (a D1 chart of GBP/USD) we can see the daily candles progressively closed towards the highs. When the candle on 13 September closed, the next daily candle opened and the market gapped higher (indicated by the arrow). The daily trend was clearly bullish so the nature of the gap could be explained by either a technical stop or a fundamental shift. On the daily charts we generally see gaps due to overnight news that is realised when the markets are closed.

The fact that the market gapped was just the beginning – it gives a reason to investigate the chart further. The gap then provided a trigger point and a significant point of interest.

The first rule of gaps is that the market does not like to see them; once a gap forms the market tries to close it. The length of time it takes to close is determined partly by what caused the gap in the first place.

Some traders do nothing but trade gaps. An edge can still exist there to some extent, but like most things in trading, if you are just finding this out now the edge is usually gone.

CHART 29: GBP/USD D1

The most interesting part of the gap for me comes at the point where the gap has attempted to close and is either closed or not. There are chart perfectionists out there who say a gap has to close to the exact pip, but personally I think if the gap has closed within the upper or lower Fibonacci retracement limits (23.6% or 61.8%) then this is usually enough for me to find it of interest.

You will develop your own style of trading gaps. There are no set rules for gap trading, just a set of options after a gap is formed.

If you sold into the gap on Chart 29 and made some profit then this is a relatively safe style of trading. I would personally be looking at this gap as a potential continuation pattern, due to the underlying trend of the market and the fact the market has gapped up.

My basic guidelines for gap trading are:

1. The trend is your friend.

2. The 80/20 rule (what moves fundamentally will trade technically).

3. Fibonacci (80% of the time a move retraces to a minimum 50%).

4. If the market can't close above/below the gap, the original underlying trend is in play and the gap is the catalyst.

Based on this reasoning I would always look to go with the overall trend once the gap has closed or made a significant attempt to close. However, it must be said that many traders just use gaps as an opportunity for them to be closed, which is a perfectly good short-term strategy.

7. Fibonacci and the significance of overextended markets

You'll already have detected from reading this far that Fibonacci is one of my favourite technical analysis tools.

Everybody who looks at the charts can see what has happened in the past. This is fact. When I use Fibonacci I am looking to select a point of interest, a specific move or a sample of data that looks important to me and therefore other traders. Once I have identified these moves I can use Fibonacci in two ways:

1. **Fibonacci retracements** – to predict how the market may move back into the range away from the highs or lows.

2. **Fibonacci expansions** – to predict how the market will extend out of the range, break with the trend and continue higher or lower.

1. Retracements

The key to using Fibonacci correctly is to identify what a strong directional move actually is. Fibonacci and the self-fulfilling nature of technical analysis will not apply if you plot Fibonacci retracements randomly on the chart.

A strong directional move will show:

1. A series of three or more candles of the same colour.

2. The candles' bodies should grow in size, indicating volume.

3. You should see candle wicks support the direction of the trend by being below or above the body.

4. You need to start from an absolute low point to a high point, or vice versa.

If you want to know where a market is going, see first where it has been. I use Fibonacci retracements on higher time frames to see where future potential activity might be.

Example

When looking at the higher time frame the monthly is king. If you start to use yearly charts you will be looking too far back; this is more for investing than intraday trading. Using the M1 chart, I find you can get a good overall picture of where the market has been and where it can potentially go in the future.

CHART 30: GBP/USD M1

As I've mentioned once or twice already, my Fibonacci principle states that 80% of the time a strong directional move will retrace to 50%. Any trading tool, indicator or strategy that can give you an 80% edge is something to pay attention to.

In Chart 30 (an M1 chart of GBP/USD) there is a strong directional move. All the points I state above as being defining criteria of a strong directional move are visible to the right-hand side of the first large vertical line.

The M1 chart provides an overview. It gives a framework and support and resistance points to use on the smaller time frame charts. We do not trade from the M1 chart itself.

Notes:

1. The first vertical line illustrates a significant high to a significant low point in the M1 chart. This is where the Fibonacci retracement is drawn from and to.

2. A longer-term view going back a number of years is taken, but where GBP/USD is currently trading holds some clues as to what can happen in the future.

3. At the second vertical line the market appeared as if it could be looking to retrace to the 50% (80% Fibonacci rule). However this was rejected and the market moved lower.

4. For an extended period of time the 23.6% Fibonacci level acted as significant support.

5. At the point of the third vertical line the market once held above the 23.6% and then more importantly found support on the 38.2% Fibonacci line. This again indicated the market may target the 50% line.

Obviously you would not sit watching this chart over this period of years, waiting for it to form. The idea is just to use the M1 chart to see what has happened in the past.

It is clear the market sold off aggressively and has not yet got back to the 50% retracement, which it does 80% of the time. There are essentially now two options:

1. Buy GBP/USD targeting the 50% level

2. Sell GBP/USD from the 50% level

This is now a good point to look to trade the market. The Fibonacci analysis on the M1 bigger picture can be applied to the smaller time frames to identify an actual trade.

Chart 31 is a zoomed in view of the GBP/USD 50% Fibonacci line on the D1.

CHART 31: GBP/USD D1

On the D1 chart the buy or sell decisions can be made a lot more accurately:

1. The market does not break the upper Bollinger band at the point where on the M1 chart the market made its third failed approach towards the 50% level.

2. There are a series of down candle closes at the top of the Bollinger band range, including a doji (reversal candle).

3. The RSI has moved away from the D1 extreme and below the overbought.

A D1 chart still gives a fairly big picture, so the actual trade calls should come from an hourly and potentially an M15 chart.

The framework was identified on the M1, confirmed on the D1, and now it's the lower time frame's job to provide the trade entry and exit points.

So let's move to an H1 chart of GBP/USD (see Chart 32). There are two clear selling opportunities, which are marked on the chart.

CHART 32: GBP/USD H1

Recap

1. Take an M1 or higher time frame view to get an idea of where the market has been and where it may potentially go.

2. Confirm this trade theory with a smaller time frame such as the D1 or H1.

3. Trade based on the indicators on the H1 or M15 using the higher time frame.

2. Expansions

Fibonacci expansions are used in the same way as retracements. A sample of previous data is used to predict where the market may move in the future. Unlike the retracements – where you look for an extended move and the market to come back into that range (to the 50%) – expansions are used to predict the unknown future.

Expansions are generally used when levels are few and far between, or when markets are making new, uncharted highs.

For example, at the time of writing the DAX is targeting 10,000. As this is a new high there is no past record on which we can form a view about the future. There are no previous higher time frame points of attraction above 10,000.

How they work

Expansions work on similar percentage points to those of Fibonacci retracements. This time you only have three levels: the 61.8%, the 100% and the 161.8% expansion levels. What you are doing is taking a previous significant move and applying the Fibonacci principles to predict a future continuation of that move.

With Fibonacci retracement you are anticipating the markets moving back into the trading range and using the 50% as a pivot or confirmation. With expansion levels you are expecting a trend continuation and the markets to break higher and lower targeting the various expansion levels mentioned.

When using an expansion I will also plot a retracement from the same points, using this to show that the direction of the market is still valid. The 50% retracement point is used as a confirmation of the trend.

In the following example using the DAX (Chart 33), I know that the 10,000 level is a major point of attraction on the upside.

CHART 33: DAX D1

I follow these six steps:

1. I take the low from 15 April as my starting point. I then take the high made on 15 May as a move that has potential to continue upwards.

2. I draw a Fibonacci expansion (lines marked FE) from these points.

3. I know the 10,000 level is a point of major significance, so the fact the 100% expansion point is above this is a good sign.

4. I draw a Fibonacci retracement from the same high and low points as the expansion (9088.14 and 9813.73). This tells me that if the market does not retrace to the 50% then there is still bullish momentum remaining in this period of trading.

5. I look for the 10,000 level and the 100% Fibonacci expansion to be the point of attraction on a continued up move.

6. I buy around a significant point of attraction from the retracement pattern, so in this case the 38.2% level is a good buy to test the expansion levels from.

Once again, by combining the tools you have available you can give yourself much more confidence in your trade calls.

Fibonacci confirmed the underlying trend by rejecting the 50% and finding support on the 38.2%. You then have clear and concise targets from the expansions that work from the same Fibonacci principles that proved the market was going up.

CHAPTER 6.

The Trading Plan

DO YOU HAVE A TRADING PLAN? YOU CERTAINLY NEED ONE.

One of the most important things when trading is deciding what you want to achieve. Like most people your answer will likely be "to make money." Very true, but without realistic and quantifiable goals you will quickly get disillusioned.

With my online trading education, it is in the areas of planning trades, mental preparation for the trading session and making use of time-saving routines where I believe I bring the most value.

I hated planning and routine myself in my early trading days. Remember, much of what is to be learnt from this book centres around what has cost me money. Save yourself this money, time and effort by cutting out my early mistakes and the mistakes I have observed in others.

After some costly reality checks early on in my trading, I, like everyone else, had to admit that it was worth having some sort of structure prior to entering the markets.

Everything in your plan should be intended to save you time and give you reassurance that you are doing the right thing, or sound a warning that you may be doing the wrong thing.

Ask yourself these questions

The questions below should help you to approach your trading as a whole and each individual trading session in the right way.

1. What type of trader are you?

Do you know? Do you care?

There are lots of trading styles that you can follow – such as swing trader, trend trader, counter-trend trader, etc. – but when it comes to your plan you are either an intraday or overnight trader.

If you hold your trades overnight you are more of an investor style of trader. On the other hand, intraday traders are looking to make the most of short-term momentum and directional moves.

My focus is on intraday trading. If you trade only when the markets are open in this way then you are looking for on average a 20 to 50 pip move at least once a day. That is what your plan should revolve around.

2. How are you holding and using your capital?

The amount of money you hold can be viewed in two ways:

1. You hold money on deposit as your finite account stop. If there is no more money then there are no more trades opened.

2. You use your account capital as margin, which you can add to, to open up multiple positions throughout the day.

I will go into this in more detail in the risk chapter, but essentially you are either using your capital for one large position or several smaller ones. Again if you don't know this how can you run stops or have a real idea of what you are risking versus what the rewards will be?

3. The time frame of your money on deposit

Does the amount of money you have on deposit have a time frame? Do you wish to hold that invested money for a set period of time in your trading account?

This forms part of what you are trying to ultimately achieve. If you are actively using that amount of money to trade then it will have a time-cost benefit.

You need to know what this is in the form of a reasonable return. Traders can fall into the trap of putting a sum of money into trading and not making or losing a significant sum, but spending hours of time at the screen. This is a cost to you.

4. Are you a technical or fundamental trader?

If you are solely one or the other then good luck. I have explained the 80/20 rule and how a balance can benefit any trader's approach.

5. What is your attitude to risk?

1. How open are you to risk; do you trade with or without a stop?

2. Do you have a set amount of price movement or a set amount of money at which point you exit when trades go against you?

3. Is risk hurting your trading style; do you constantly get stopped out?

If you can't tell me the answer to these questions then you have probably not been trading a sustainable plan and therefore not to your full potential.

Why questioning yourself is so important

The importance of these questions is so that you obtain an overview of what you are trying to achieve as a trader. Without realistic goals you will get frustrated very quickly. The amount of effort and stress invested will not equate to the return you achieve.

Goals

I have mentioned the importance of trading goals. Here are some easy steps to help set your goals:

1. Write down your goals and when you analyse your trades look back to these. What is the correlation between what you set out to achieve and what you achieved in practice?

2. The rules you need to put in place to meet your individual needs and goals are down to you. I can give you an idea but the rules have to come from you.

3. I could not be your risk manager unless I knew all your answers to the risk questions. It's down to you to think about your answers and act on them. You have to be your own complete trading team, so you are your own risk manager.

4. Your goals have to be individual to you and they have to be honest. If they are not then you are only giving yourself false parameters to work from and ultimately you will never achieve them.

My typical trading goal

I don't use a complicated plan. I just want to make 5% to 10% of my account, or between £500 and £1000 on a trade (based on my average balance and margin of £10k).

I do this by:

1. Understanding the fundamental drivers acting within the markets at a given time.

2. Trading only technical levels and areas that are of interest on my charts.

3. Knowing I am willing to lose £500 to prove my trade call is correct.

4. Sticking firmly to this plan.

That's how simple my trading goals are. This is of course after years of trading, risk management and mentoring. You will have to put a little effort into the exact make up of your plan and goals to reach this point.

Use facts in your plan

Make use of facts in your trading plan. These will be facts to do with the markets and facts about yourself. Everything you put into your trading plan should then revolve around these facts. Like your charts and technical analysis, there should not be so much information that it becomes complicated or a distraction.

Facts from the market

Here are the facts you need from the market for your plan:

Key data

This contributes to the underlying fundamental sentiment of the markets.

This is as simple as opening up an economic calendar. Bloomberg and Reuters both have free access to this data and so does Forex Street (FXstreet.com), which I personally think is the best source.

You hopefully already know how to read the calendar and (from what I have told you earlier) what is important to focus on. I would take the whole week of figures and put them down as your starting point. List them in date order, making sure you correspond the time of the announcement or data release with your local time zone.

Key levels

I have gone through the all time frame trading approach and this is the best way of getting meaningful levels. You can of course use key pivots or significant time period highs and lows.

The point of these levels is that they should be in the products you trade regularly and should be something you will base a trade decision on.

Unscheduled events

There will be major news events that fall outside of the scheduled key data releases and speakers.

These can be the biggest money makers in trading, so on the rare occasion they happen you should have a basic idea of how to trade them. In essence, if the event is a threat to the West – a terrorist attack for example – then you buy gold and sell major indices.

Facts from yourself

Here are the facts you need from yourself for your plan:

Overall goals

Make some goals that you want to achieve from your daily, weekly and monthly sessions. The weekly and monthly goals are important, as well as the trade-by-trade goals and daily goals so that you have a view of the bigger picture. One day's trading should not make you or break you.

You will soon find that if you stick to achieving goals in smaller blocks, suddenly weeks and months have passed by and you are starting to see the benefits of your planning. Saying you want to make £100 a day, and getting somewhere close to that goal, can mean you have made £2000 in a month, so £12,000 in six months. When you actually see this happen you start to believe in your trading ability.

When you look at your account day to day and you see small fluctuations this is where you get disheartened. It's all about the long game and the targets you are working towards.

Individual trade goals

The individual goals come from your bigger picture targets. They have to fit in line with them.

Don't try and push them too hard. Profit is profit. You will get days when it is ridiculously easy to make money. You will also get days where you wonder why you ever thought trading was a good idea! It's all about smoothing that expectation curve.

Summary

It is a good idea to have all of this written down. You can use spreadsheets, Word documents, or anything that you think will bring value to your planning.

Putting some daily, weekly and monthly goals down will focus your mind and should allow you to get into trades with the correct amount and bank winners.

Knowing the fundamental data the market expects in your trading session is important. The technical levels are also good practice and your plan should keep you aware of these at all times.

If you do nothing more than set yourself a tick, percentage or monetary daily, weekly and monthly goal after reading this book, I feel I will have done enough to justify writing it.

CHAPTER 7.

The Ruff Guide
to Risk

I WILL START THIS SECTION WITH A MOMENT IN MY CAREER that changed my attitude to risk forever. This is something I am writing with my trader's hat on.

From my trader's perspective

RUFF TIP

I found it very difficult to take losing trades early on in my career, as most traders do. I developed a way of justifying the loss by saying to myself:

I am paying the market based on my own advice and decision to trade. Even though the trade may be a losing one, I have paid an amount of money, set by me, to the market for the possibility of making my potential profit.

If you think about this in a rational way and try to turn a complete negative into a somewhat positive, you may have a better time with the subject of risk.

As a professional trader my opinion of the risk department was always a negative one. The traders were the good guys doing their job and the risk team were the enemy trying to hinder their trading.

From my risk manager's perspective

In some respects you can understand this thinking; the word risk is associated with bad things. If you were a trader and got a call from me when I was a professional risk manager, it was rarely good news. If I came on the floor to speak to you it was never good news.

From my risk manager's perspective, stopping a trader out was probably much more stressful at times than trading itself, so myself and anyone in the risk team wanted traders to win just as much as the traders did.

The job of a risk manager is to help to take the emotion away from the trader and the situation. To look at the trade for what it is. Even professional traders will get on the wrong side of a trade and take huge amounts of risk for relatively small potential rewards.

A good risk manager aims to stop traders getting to this point in the first place. Risk management is a thankless job. Very much like compliance teams at banks, risk managers are an essential part of trading, but no one really likes them.

What risk management means to the retail trader

As a retail trader you are the trader and the risk manager. This means you have to be at one with both aspects: the ability to make money and also the ability to control yourself from losing too much. If you trade without an idea of risk you are simply gambling. Risk management should therefore mean the steps you take to preserve your capital. Without funds you can't trade.

There are many books and internet sources with information about trading risk. Invariably they will all contain the same generic thinking. They are usually written by people who have no skin in the game and have probably only traded very small retail accounts. They will not have experienced all the things I have, which I draw my risk conclusions from.

Too many times when you Google risk and trading you will get the same standard answer:

Risk no more than 1% to 2% of your capital on each trade.

Essentially this is a stop of 1% to 2% for a trade, based on your capital on deposit. This is fine. If you do this you will either have a prolonged and boring career in trading, or you will blow up your account very quickly.

I say prolonged and boring because you will not make very much money from trading in this way. The amount of money you would need to hold in your account to run this level of risk would be too high for the average retail trader.

Once you get bored and make one very bad trade you will more than likely wipe a significant proportion of your capital. I have seen this many times and I've done it myself. Traders want to ultimately make money. They understand the risk management rules they've set, but in reality no trader ever sticks to them 100% of the time.

If you feel you are not getting enough, in monetary terms, then you will eventually take a big risk based on fundamental data or a key level. These big-risk trades generally do not end well.

RUFF TIP

The volatility in the markets makes it practically impossible when intraday trading to pick the perfect entry point to withstand a 1% stop.

Think back to the types of human and types of trader. The amount of short-term manipulation that can be injected into the market has led to the creation of the terms:

• Stop grabber

• Pin bar

• Stop hunter

• Short/Long squeeze

Have you ever experienced one of these when intraday trading?

How I teach risk

Having read the above statement about risk, does this sound like you? Do you use a 1% to 2% stop on your trades?

I thought so.

I do teach the 1% rule and also risk-reward ratios. This is so people have an understanding of what other traders will be basing their risk profiles on. When you see a large move intraday in any product, you know that a lot of retail traders are at 1% risk. Any big move will knock a large proportion of traders out of positions. My approach to risk is more simplified.

When you put a trade on, it instantly becomes your world, you get married to the trade and you make irrational emotional decisions based on that one moment in time. This is something that takes a long time to learn to control, if indeed you ever do.

What I have found to be a better approach for intraday trading is to set a weekly loss limit. This way you can then alter your risk parameters per individual trade. If you lose all your weekly money on one trade, then you have to stop for that week.

Sounds a little too simplistic?

Try it for yourself. Losing a weekly stop in one trade will hurt you, but should still mean you remain in the game. The best lessons in trading come from pain. Losing money is that real pain you need to experience sometimes to really appreciate the trading rules.

Ratios of risk

By using a framework of risk and reward combined with daily and weekly stops, you are giving yourself rules to follow. They are your rules, so you can break them, but unlike a professional trader with a risk team to watch out for them, you have to watch out for yourself.

How many times have you pulled a stop, then continued to lose more on a trade, only to say to yourself afterwards, "I wish I had not done that."

It hopefully goes without saying that when choosing an amount of capital to use for trading purposes you should always be able to afford to lose that amount. There is also no point trading outside your comfort zone. By this I mean if you ever find yourself saying "I'll just go for it," with a larger size than you can handle, the outcome is rarely good.

The risk-reward ratios work as they give you an idea of what you think a good trade is. If you want to make £1000, would you risk £2000 to make it? That would be a negative risk-reward ratio. You risk twice as much as you are going to make (1:2).

How about risking £500 to make £1000 or £2000? Sounds more palatable. This is simply running a ratio of 2:1 or 4:1.

Over the years, rather than running fixed stops I have always advocated using ratios to give yourself an idea of what each trade means in real terms. If you are always risking more than you make, eventually you will be in trouble.

Averaging or scaling into products

I touch on this subject a lot when I talk about my own risk-reward and trading style:

1. I do not use physical stops.

2. I always start with a small initial trade.

3. I always buy or sell more if the position goes against me.

4. I buy or sell areas of value, not individual prices.

The idea behind this goes back to people and the way the professionals see the markets compared to the way retail traders see them.

From everything I have spoken about – the fundamental movement and the technical movement – I usually have a good idea where the extremes of the markets are likely to be intraday. What I therefore do is build a position of a number of trades with increasing size to fade out this inevitable squeeze.

For example, Chart 34 is an M15 of USD/CAD. This provides an example of how I would average into a short position.

CHART 34: USD/CAD M15

Here are the steps I follow:

1. I know the trend is down and I want to go short.

2. The first downward arrow is the previous high. This is where I would look to place the stop in my monetary view if I am wrong. I don't use a physical stop.

3. If I am selling I am always selling into an up candle – selling high.

4. I know the extremes the market expects from the RSI, Bollinger Bands, and support and resistance.

5. I sell multiple positions even though the market is going up between 1.23037 and 1.23174. This is called averaging into a position. Selling a price area, not one individual price.

6. When my average position is at an amount I am comfortable with I then prepare for the sell off to the key area of interest at 1.22584 (marked with the line), which is where my profit targets are set.

I can use all the above points on a shorter time frame chart to confirm my thinking, as below where Chart 35 shows an M5 USD/CAD chart with Bollinger Bands, RSI, and zoomed in support and resistance.

CHART 35: USD/CAD M5

Trading this way you can use your margin to greater effect. You can ride out market volatility and negate the need for a physical stop.

This is another idea of how to think differently about risk. I don't necessarily recommend this way of trading for everyone, since it took me years of experience as a risk manager and a trader to settle on this approach.

Trading figures and risk

Now you need to set an amount of money that allows you to achieve your trading goal.

The point of this is that it has to be realistic to what you, and only you, are trying to achieve. As I don't know your goals, I don't know your risk attitude, strategy or what type of person and trader you are, I can't dictate this for you.

The fact of the matter is that data will move the markets quickly. This injects fear and the element of time. How long can you stand firm when you know you are right, but your P&L is showing red? This is the main aim of the market over data: to make you think you are wrong.

The best way to trade data is to set a monetary stop. There is very little point using actual stops as due to volatility you will invariably get stopped out. So simply use a ratio and say "I want to risk £100 to make £200," a 2:1 risk reward ratio. Or set a daily or weekly target amount.

Everything you make from data should be treated as a bonus. Markets move 20% of the time due to fundamentals so the majority of your trading profits should come from the 80% technical trade calls.

Risk conclusions

By significantly reducing your interaction with the markets you are putting the trading odds back in your favour. The more you trade, the more spread and other costs you pay, and the lower your overall winning ratio is likely to be.

If you use the principle of a weekly stop you give yourself much more chance of winning, by being able to average into a trade or to control your stop.

PART II.
Practical Strategies

CHAPTER 8.
Reversals and Breakouts

I HAVE EXPLAINED HOW TO GO THROUGH CHARTS AND PICK out significant points of interest. These will generally come from the higher time frame charts. I have demonstrated how you can look at the past to get a framework for the intraday charts and for your trading ideas.

When looking for trading opportunities from a technical perspective, being able to identify key turning points in a market is very useful. In this chapter we will look at catching tops, bottoms and breakouts.

I categorise these strategies as:

1. Bull and bear reversals

2. Bull and bear breakouts

1. Bull and bear reversals

The first part of this strategy involves looking over the various time frames for periods where the market could have found its extremes. I use a combination of DeM and RSI to establish if a market is significantly overbought or oversold, and so due a reversal.

The higher the time frame the more significant the signal, but the more time it may take to filter though for an intraday trade or signal.

The monthly chart is always a good place to start as this holds the most data. I would not go any higher than this and you should resist the temptation to look at too much historical data.

As I have explained, DeM and RSI look similar, but taking DeM extremes and correlating these with the RSI overbought/oversold levels gives a much clearer signal than looking at either of these two indicators individually.

Chart 36 is an M1 chart of the DAX showing the extreme highs and lows, and DeM and RSI indicators.

CHART 36: DAX M1

From studying DeM and RSI we can see that there is a double top in the DeM and that the extremes of the bull move seem to have been reached. This again is why I put a tolerance into most of the oscillator-based indicators to fade out any over-extensions you may get beyond the known industry standard settings.

DeM (0.75) has much further to go to get down to the midpoint (0.5 and 50) than the RSI (66.9) and this can lead to an accelerated injection of downward bias as the oscillators look to sync up.

From here we have to zoom into the more actionable shorter time frames and do some additional technical analysis to pick a trade entry.

When the markets are close to the extremes of both DeM and RSI the trend is clearly confirmed as a strong bull trend. However, sooner or later this trend will end.

When you have a very strong uptrend you will get a short-term dip as buyers come in to trade for that short-term value. When trading a trend you have to assess the time factor. A lot can happen in an hour, day, week and month. Identifying a trend by using indicators and oscillators takes a fair amount of time due to their lagging nature. To confirm any strong trend this will have to be taken into consideration.

Chart 37 is the D1 DAX showing the extreme highs and lows, and DeM and RSI indicators.

The monthly view has led us to a possible point of further investigation. We now have to focus on what the smaller time frames tell us in order to actually put a trade on.

We plot the chart in the same way, looking for an indication on the daily chart for when the monthly correction will filter through to the market. We see two periods (vertical lines) of where DeM hits the standard 0.7 reversal point and 0.8 extreme, and note how RSI shows divergence and can't print above 70 at both these points.

By drawing a simple trend line on the daily candles we can see the market still wants to push higher, even though the monthly DeM and RSI have shown a reversal and the daily DeM and RSI are heading to the midpoint. It is only when the market closes on the trend line and then below it that the market indicates it may be ready to trade lower and correct the up move.

CHART 37: DAX D1

RUFF TIP

This is a technical break as the close of where the down move started acted as resistance when the market sold off. This shows it is a technical sell-off; if it had been due to fundamentals there would most likely have been a gap.

We have taken a monthly signal with a daily confirmation and now we have to trade this opportunity. This means zooming in the chart once again, this time to the hourly. Chart 38 shows the H1 DAX with the extreme highs and lows, and DeM and RSI indicators.

CHART 38: DAX H1

As all the signals in higher-time frames indicate sell, we have to look for the high point of the hourly chart to act as a potential entry point.

The first entry point is the break of the daily trend line (marked with the thumbs up symbol). See how the market breaks then consolidates before trying to push up higher and squeeze out the short positions (think of those working to 1% risk).

Once the market then breaks lower it is not until we see a spike up in DeM, almost to the 0.7 reversal point, where we can once again sell high and sell into further down movement (second thumbs up symbol).

This is why it is important to have both DeM and RSI when trading as you may have liquidated shorts, or even bought, if you'd been trading solely on DeM. The fact the RSI remains relatively unchanged and steady towards the oversold level gives you an indication this is still a downtrend.

2. Bull and bear breakouts

The bull and bear breakouts are the other extreme to reversals. They work around the midpoint. This is where the market does not exhibit a strong trend and has small candle bodies, indicating it is ready to choose a new trend and breakout in one direction.

These are a little more difficult to identify. They still rely on DeM and RSI levels, but you are trying to use the midpoint (50) as a potential breakout area. I have explained before about the DeM oscillator being more of a lead indicator and showing the extremes. So what we are trying to do is trade one lead oscillator from another.

I would class these types of trade setups as purely intraday, so the hourly chart is probably the best time frame to do this on. If you try and go for the longer time frames you will invariably get into the trade too early and risk getting squeezed out. As this is a breakout trade we are concentrating on finding a formation that shows relatively small candle bodies in a tight range.

Chart 39 is the H1 EUR/USD with DeM and RSI, and with extra extreme levels plotted.

CHART 39: EUR/USD H1

Notes:

1. The DeM shows the extremes much more clearly than the RSI in my opinion. So we are looking for the lead indicator to show us that a potential move is coming, and that the breakout of the current range is imminent.

2. We see very little movement in the RSI, which is ranging around the midpoint. DeM breaks aggressively from the bull reversal to bear reversal with no real significance in the candle direction or in the RSI. This is a precursor to a bullish breakout.

3. Following the spike in DeM, we look to RSI to catch up to the lead indicator and bring more bullish momentum and buyers into the market.

4. More people trade from RSI than DeM, so as RSI gathers momentum there will be more buyers attracted into the market, pushing it higher.

5. We then see RSI target the overbought 70 mark, by which time DeM has started to trade towards the 0.8 extreme.

Conclusion

This is another example of how oscillators can be used in similar ways to achieve similar trade ideas. The whole point of this is that you have to identify if the current market trend is ranging or trending and then tailor your strategy around this.

- The **reversal works well in strong trending markets**.

- **Breakouts work specifically well in trending markets**.

You have to pay attention to the time frame and also the expected trade outcome.

CHAPTER 9.

Identifying Overextended Markets and Trading the Key 50%

FIBONACCI IS A VERY POWERFUL TOOL WHEN USED correctly. Here I describe how to build a trading strategy around the key 50% retracement level.

Before you draw any Fibonacci levels, you have to understand what you want to achieve. Are you looking for value, direction or confirmation?

Identifying a strong directional move, depending on the time frame, will give you an idea of where the market will have found value in the past and where it could potentially then trade to in the future.

By identifying the strong directional or overextended market, I have been able to incorporate the Fibonacci studies and more importantly build strategies around the key levels.

In this chapter we will look at:

1. Strong directional moves.

2. Overextended candles.

3. Fibonacci expansions.

1. Strong directional moves

The first step is to identify a strong market move. This is easier than many people think. By using the candle bodies you can see when the market has found a solid trend and where the direction of the market sentiment has been dominant in one direction.

Take Chart 40, a weekly chart for the EUR/JPY. It shows a Fibonacci retracement on what I class as a directional move.

CHART 40: EUR/JPY

From the upwards arrow and the start of trading on the weekly chart there are seven up candles making consecutive higher highs. I think it is clear to say that this is a strong, directional uptrend.

The fact that the eighth weekly candle does not make a new high means we have a set period of time and movement to use in order to predict what the market could do in the future.

I have said that any strong directional move will retrace 80% of the time to 50%. (If you don't know this off by heart by now then you need to read this book again!) A fact of trading is that a 70% to 80% edge is all you are ever likely to get from any technical analysis.

But much of the time it is what the markets have *not* done that is important. So if a move doesn't retrace, or doesn't look like retracing at all, then usually the underlying trend prevails and the market carries on in that direction.

For this particular strong directional move, we are using the Fibonacci retracement to go with the percentage. Anticipating that what goes up will come down, we are working on the basis that this scenario will follow the rule that 80% of the time there is a retracement to 50%.

This is a weekly move, so this is a trade setup that will take time to present a tradable opportunity. This also ties in with the all time frame method of trading, taking an easy-to-identify move and then incorporating the self-fulfilling nature of technical analysis.

We can then zoom into the smaller time frames in order to identify real-time potential trades. Once we have the high and low of the seven weekly candle formation we can draw our Fibonacci retracement from the low to the high of the move. This will give us the key 50% retracement level and all the other key areas of interest based on the directional up movement.

After the weekly view I would then look to the daily and hourly charts to build a picture of how I could benefit from the potential retracement. We could also pick out key weekly and daily levels from the candlesticks to give ourselves other key areas of interest and potential trigger points.

Once EUR/JPY reaches the high point and makes no significant attempt to test higher, we need to look to the daily charts to identify areas for further investigation. Chart 41 shows the D1 of EUR/JPY.

Obviously even at the top of a very strong bull run there may still be attempts to pull buyers back into the market. At the top of the daily chart there are three full days (highlighted by the box in the top left-hand corner of chart) of consolidation after the high is made. This is a good sign as on the back of such a strong up move if the bulls wanted to test higher this would likely have been attempted by now. Use your understanding of candlesticks and see how the upper wicks indicate upside weakness.

CHART 41: EUR/JPY D1

Notes:

1. On the daily chart, 144.933 is a key area of interest where the market can potentially look to turn. Once the area of consolidation breaks, the market does head lower. We can see by the size of the candle body that there is a lot of volume and momentum brought into the market at this point.

2. We are again looking at the daily charts and in relation to the other candles this is a large daily sell off (we can class this as an overextended candle).

3. We can tell this is a technical break as the 143.257 acts as support then resistance when the second overextended candle opens the next day. We know now that Fibonacci levels should play some part in the future trading.

4. Once we close below 143.257, at the daily level, for the foreseeable future this only ever acts as a point of resistance.

5. We know that the trade we are focusing on is to get short to the 50% retracement level. From a longer-term day trade (with overnights) you could quite easily short the 143.257 with a stop of 144.933 and target the 50%. You could even short the 23.6% with a stop of 143.257. These two trades would give you in excess of a 1:2 or 1:4 risk-reward ratio respectively.

However, as I like to minimise risk, I am looking for an intraday trade. This of course will take longer for the right trade to present itself, but as we have done the majority of the hard work identifying the trade I now just have to use the 50% as the target and the hourly chart to find the best entry point. I don't really get excited about this trade setup until the higher Fibonacci retracement points start to work on the smaller time frame and act as resistance.

Chart 42 shows the H1 of EUR/JPY.

CHART 42: EUR/JPY H1

On the hourly time frame we can start to identify opportunities:

1. After the market breaks the daily level of 144.933 we can see how future levels act as points of attraction.

2. The daily level of 143.257 becomes a very strong area of interest for the hourly candles. We see intraday highs and consolidation. The 23.6% retracement level is the next logical down point of support, so any short would see that as a potential exit point.

3. The 23.6% retracement level acts as a pivot for future trading for some time. Although we would not have made nearly as much profit as we would from selling on the daily charts, this is a relatively low-risk trade with defined boundaries for a stop and exit. This is a perfect setup for intraday trading.

The real opportunities come later when we can start to draw studies on the hourly chart that encapsulate the current movement. Remember, once you have made money intraday you not only have confidence this Fibonacci framework is viable, but until you hit the 50% you have plenty of trading opportunities.

In this example there is the simple trend channel that funnels the hourly candles and trading direction from the 23.6% retracement level to the 38.2% level and finally to our first touch of the 50% target level. This is where you can define stronger entry points and exit points for more intraday trades.

Chart 43 shows an H1 of EUR/JPY with a trend channel.

This is where it is time to cash in on your patience.

Once the hourly trend channel holds (again, it does not necessarily have to be perfect), we have the ability to sell to the high of the range knowing that the lower points of attraction are working from our higher time frame directional move.

Once the 50% is hit we may see a bounce and we may see increased selling momentum. Regardless, the strong directional move and the Fibonacci framework have provided plenty of opportunities to sell into the intraday down moves.

CHART 43: EUR/JPY H1

2. Overextended candles

This principle of the overextended candle works in the same way as the strong directional market; indeed, a strong directional move will generally contain these types of candle. These moves, however, are much more based on short-term activity. When there is a large technical break, or an overextended candle whose body trades significantly more than the current range, then this once again is a situation where we can use Fibonacci.

The key is identifying a breakout candle which is much larger in volume and body than other previous candles. Our focus here is on the candlestick body, as the wicks can be misleading when using Fibonacci in this sort of setup.

In this example we will see an overextended candle in GBP/USD. We can see that the next relevant down candle only had a body of 32 ticks and the extended candle had a body of 63 ticks, so twice volume and real body amount.

I have included the ATR (average true range), which calculates the average previous trading activity. I only really use this for illustration; I don't think you can predict a potential breakout candle from ATR, but it does confirm the continuation by the way of resistance becoming support at key ATR points.

Chart 44 is the H1 of GBP/USD, showing a strong directional candle.

CHART 44: GBP/USD H1

The important steps are:

1. The key to a strong directional move is to identify something that looks out of the ordinary.

2. As this is a quick movement we are looking for a continuation pattern, not a reversal. We use the 50% and other Fibonacci levels as confirmation that the overall trend will continue, not retrace. As long as the market does not retrace or test the lower Fibonacci levels, especially the 50%, the uptrend will resume and the market will make new highs.

3. The key is also to draw the Fibonacci from the opposite direction of the extended candle. In this case the candle is a bull candle (an up candle), so

you need to draw the Fibonacci retracement from the high to the low to get the extension levels as potential targets.

4. In this case the 161.8% is a good indication of where the move will get to. You could draw a Fibonacci expansion from the low to the high of the extended candle, but this never works as well.

5. This of course is a short-term trade as we are using the hourly chart. You are looking for a quick continuation and to take your profit within the close of that day. There will be patterns like this that consolidate for only one candle and then go on to make new highs.

Once you can identify overextended candles this will be a high percentage trade you can use.

3. Fibonacci expansions

Fibonacci expansions are a useful tool when there are no previous levels on which to base your trades.

For example, this is the case at the time of writing for major indices. The DAX has hit 10,000 but the FTSE and S&P have not yet hit the round numbers of 7,000 and 2,000 respectively. By combining the Fibonacci retracement and the Fibonacci expansion you can get a good idea of how markets will move when there is no technical data available.

Let's look at the FTSE. We look for a strong directional move and plot the Fibonacci retracement as normal. Chart 45 shows the D1 with the key 50% Fibonacci retracement point.

On this daily chart we can see that after the sell off the lower 61.8% and key 50% act as support.

We can see how the FTSE is consolidating between the new highs and the 50% retracement.

The overall trend is bullish, so if we are going to make new highs what would be the target?

CHART 45: FTSE 100 D1

We follow these steps:

1. We can draw a Fibonacci expansion from the key 50% to that previous high. This way we get two targets of 6964.77, just below the key psychological 7,000 mark. We also then get an upper level of attraction at 7073.46. (With the benefit of hindsight we know the FTSE has now hit this level.)

2. As this is a daily chart you could then move to the hourly to start to pick a low point in order to trade to these upper targets. As more and more of the Fibonacci retracement levels act as support, the more likely it is that the market will test and break to new highs and target the Fibonacci expansion levels.

3. Fibonacci expansion levels work very well on previous movements, but, like the retracement, are notoriously difficult to plot correctly. By using the Fibonacci 50% and a previous (all-time) high to draw the expansion, I have found I get much more consistent results.

CHAPTER 10.

Gaps

THERE ARE TWO WAYS TO TRADE GAPS:

1. A reversal and gap close.

2. A continuation of the trend and the gap direction.

The majority of technical analysts regard gaps as a point on the chart that should be closed. This is a good strategy, but fairly one-dimensional. Unless you are looking at charts constantly there is a strong possibility you will miss a gap forming.

Referring back to my 80/20 rule, I like to understand why a gap formed and then identify a way of trading it. As with the big moves after data releases, there is just as much profit to be made from trading *after* a gap, rather than trading the gap itself.

Whether a gap is significant or not can be determined by how long it takes to make an attempt to close:

- If the **market makes little attempt to close the gap**, and continues to aggressively move in the gap direction, then clearly the underlying sentiment of the market has not changed.

- If the **gap is closed relatively quickly**, in a few hourly candles, then the market has discounted this news or event and will return to parity, or will start to retrace and reverse the gap direction.

Chart 46 shows the H1 of GBP/USD, with a gap to the upside. I have indicated the daily levels on this hourly chart using vertical lines, to illustrate how long the gap took to close.

CHART 46: GBP/USD H1

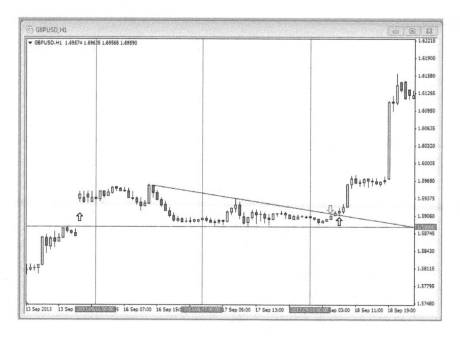

Although the gap was never closed to the pip, it was near enough. After taking almost a full day of trading to approach the trigger point, this tells us two things:

1. The market has taken its time to absorb the information, so it must have had some relevance to the markets.

2. The underlying uptrend is still technically sound.

The type of trader you are now comes into question. If you are a scalper – a short-term trader – then you may want to sell the highs back to the trigger point. This is a perfectly good trade idea. If you want to scalp with the underlying trend then you are looking for short-term bounces at, or close to, the 1.58860 trigger point (taken from the high of the daily gap candle) and buying to resistance (indicated by the diagonal line).

The difference between a position trader and a scalper is time. If you can hold overnight positions, you are by definition a position trader. If you can't then you are scalping intraday movements while the markets are open. It is that simple. In either case, you are looking for the momentum which will give you the direction and ability to maximise the profit from your trade entry point.

After the gap the market naturally moves down due to profit-taking on the gap. However, as this is over many hourly candles it does not show a great deal of momentum or panic. This indicates to me that the more the trigger point acts as an area of interest and support, the more likely we are to see a reaction to the gap continuing from the existing trend.

What we don't see in the price action can often be more powerful than what we do see. For example, after this gap we saw little attempt to move up, but also very slow moving direction trading downwards to close the gap.

We also never actually technically close the gap to the pip. As the trend of the market is up, and the gap has for all intents and purposes closed, the daily trigger point is now acting as support on the short-term hourly charts. From here we are looking for another indication that the bullish nature and trend of the market will continue.

This is where the theory of combining your technical analysis comes into practice. Chart 47 is the H1 of GBP/USD again with a Fibonacci retracement based on the previous market trading and a Fibonacci expansion based on the gap. You can see the gap to the upside and the subsequent trend continuation.

CHART 47: GBP/USD H1

At this point you should re-evaluate the trading rules that you know to work and answer them before you trade. These will tell you if your trade idea is confirmed.

1. The trend is your friend

The previous trading action in the market is bullish. The hourly candles are making higher lows and the gap broke to the highs, all indicating bullish sentiment. Trade call: BUY.

2. The 80/20 rule: what moves fundamentally will trade technically

The potentially fundamental gap will trade within technical boundaries and will adhere to technical studies. The lows of the market provide consistent support of the trigger point. Trade call: BUY.

3. Fibonacci – 80% of the time a move retraces to 50%

The Fibonacci levels are drawn from 1.57830 to 1.59632, with 50% at 1.58730. Any strong directional move (including a gap) will retrace to the 50% Fibonacci level 80% of the time. The 50% has held. This chart clearly indicates the 50% had not been hit and therefore the market is still bullish. Trade call: BUY.

The key to understanding this 80% approach is defining the extended move. In this case you could use the gap itself to plot a Fibonacci retracement, but I would personally incorporate the previous up move and where I deemed the bullish momentum to have originated from. If we fail to retrace to the 50% point, or test and do not close below it, then the original trend which is bullish is still more prevalent and the market should then rise and attempt to make a new high.

This is my interpretation and how I view the markets; in time you will develop your own opinions. Most of your future success in using technical analysis will come from the confidence you have in using the tools at your disposal. There is always an element of self-doubt when you are using technical analysis; worrying that you are wrong or, more often, that you can't be right. The art of trading is to have the correct balance of belief and repetition.

By using these three rules to identify a potential trade we have established the trend is bullish and we are looking for a buy.

Another rule we can use is as follows:

4. If a gap can't close above/below the trigger point, the original underlying trend is in play and the trigger point is a potential entry.

The 1.58860 trigger point on the hourly chart has been significant support and the market has not closed below it.

From here we have no doubt that we are looking for a break to the upside and we need to buy low. In this case we have a great level in the trigger point. What we are now looking for is the market to regain the bullish momentum and to move higher.

This is where the Fibonacci expansion comes into play. Often if you have no defined upper levels then the expansion levels can be used to predict future points of interest based on previous market movement. In this instance we have the gap.

Chart 48 is the H1 of GBP/USD with a gap to the upside, showing how Fibonacci expansions can be a target.

CHART 48: GBP/USD H1

By taking the Fibonacci expansion from the trigger point (1.58860) to the next traded price (1.59632), we can predict via the expansion levels where potential interest points may be on the upside. Of course, we do not know what will happen in the market after the initial gap, but we know the market has a memory and any fundamental gap will trade technically. (Refer back to the Fibonacci section for a refresher.)

This may seem a long-winded procedure, but basically you are identifying an opportunity from the daily chart gap. Once the gap has formed you are taking the initial break and trigger point as a point of attraction and assessing if or how the market will close this gap from the shorter hourly time frame.

If you are satisfied you understand what the market is telling you from the gap and the subsequent trading, you can look at ways to enter the market. You could simply buy at the gap and hold on, but that is not without its risks. Both position traders and scalpers are ultimately looking for momentum here.

Gap trading will invariably be down to some new element of news. Once you understand what caused the gap you can trade it with the 80/20 rule. Always pay attention to the underlying trend and also what the gap direction means to both short-term traders and longer-term investors. A gap makes every type of trader investigate the charts further.

Chart 49 shows the H1 GBP/USD with the gap to the upside and consolidation before trend continuation.

Now that you have a clean chart with key points of interest, you can get a trade setup that suits the strategy conclusion we came to: buy.

- Fibonacci expansion 100%: 1.59632
- Fibonacci expansion 161.8%: 1.59746
- Trigger point: 1.58860
- Trend line down starting: 1.59632
- Trend line up starting: 1.57830
- 14 period RSI

The trend lines are most important on this chart as they are drawn from the hourly perspective and they show the support and resistance the market has found. The Fibonacci expansion levels are drawn from the daily gap. We know the trigger point is holding as support and where the two trend lines meet we could see a potential break out trade to the upside.

When the market meets the two trend lines we see a typical technical trend line break. This is where the trend line is broken to the upside. The market then uses this as support and bounces higher, signified by the arrows.

CHART 49: GBP/USD H1

RUFF TIP

How do you tell a technical gap from a fundamental move? Generally speaking, a technical break will test the prior break point as support or resistance in the next candle. Whereas a fundamental move will either gap or make no attempt to retest any break points.

Once the market breaks out of the trend line then the daily Fibonacci expansion points become relevant and can act as the next point of attraction.

It is worth noting that prior to the break RSI was steadily rising to the 70 mark, which is considered overbought. The RSI then remains above 70 and as the market breaks the trend lines it gathers momentum and then targets the 100% expansion level.

If you bought the break that is a 56 tick winner.

It is interesting to note that when the market hits the 100% expansion the RSI finds support on the 70 RSI level. The market then ranges between the 100% and 161.8% expansion levels before the RSI once again rises (91) leading to a huge breakout past the 161.8% and up to a range almost 150 ticks higher.

Conclusion

THERE IS A REASON WHY I BEGAN THIS BOOK WITH A LOT OF theory. There is not only a lot to know about trading, but infinite ways to explain it. From all the traders I have met and taught, the clear observation I have made is that although they have the basic human needs, traders see the markets differently and they absolutely approach life differently.

When you immerse yourself in the markets you have to understand the rules of the game.

Only by asking yourself truthful questions can you ascertain what you are trying to achieve and if you are going about trading in the correct manner. To be a successful trader it's not always about knowing more than the next guy, it's about knowing yourself and how you function in this complex and challenging environment.

Trading is not about being right on the direction of the market. It is about being right at the precise time the markets move in that direction. Having an opinion on longer-term direction is only suitable for certain types of traders and maybe more so for longer-term investors. Having an opinion when day trading can very expensive.

Look to the past to predict the future. Buy low and sell high. Keep in mind my 80/20 rule of trading. You can't simply trade technically and ignore the fundamentals, no matter what anyone else tells you.

Enjoy your trading, learn from my approach and my mistakes… and good luck.

Steve Ruffley

SEE THE MARKETS THROUGH THE EYES OF A PRO

iView Charts

All the concepts for my charts and technical studies
are in my software, iView Charts:

www.iViewcharts.com/Ruffguide

Lightning Source UK Ltd.
Milton Keynes UK
UKHW020810160421
382087UK00004B/317